For the
Beauty
of the
Church

FOR THE
BEAUTY
OF THE
CHURCH

Casting a Vision for the Arts

EDITED BY **W. DAVID O. TAYLOR**

BakerBooks

a division of Baker Publishing Group
Grand Rapids, Michigan

Published by Baker Books
a division of Baker Publishing Group
P.O. Box 6287, Grand Rapids, MI 49516-6287
www.bakerbooks.com

Printed in the United States of America

Library of Congress Cataloging-in-Publication Data
For the beauty of the church : casting a vision for the arts / [compiled by]
W. David O. Taylor.
    p. cm.
Includes bibliographical references.
ISBN 978-0-8010-7191-1 (pbk.)
 1. Christianity and the arts. 2. Art and religion. I. Taylor, W. David O.,
1972–
BR115.A8F66 2010
261.57—dc22   2009037738

10   11   12   13   14   15   16   7   6   5   4   3   2   1

To the beloved community of artists at Hope Chapel
throughout the years
and
to the beloved community of artists everywhere

Contents

Foreword

Partnership? Companionship? Coinherence? I'm trying to find the term that best tells how beauty and art interlink and infuse each other with meaning.

Beauty is always available. It is there to be attended to, and art is our human response to whatever we see as beautiful. Not the kind of beauty we might call pretty or decorative—it can be strong, shocking, confusing, boundary-breaking, thrusting forward in experimental ways—but beauty that most often reflects glory, the glory of our God who created us with the capacity for recognizing, responding, and receiving beauty through the work of artists. It is an imperative, particularly for artists who call themselves Christian believers, to glorify God in their creative lives.

This role of the arts has not always been received kindly in Christian churches. Often art has been seen as too experimental, too self-indulgent, or too disturbing to be recognized as a gift of grace. Perhaps this was one of the disjunctions David Taylor had in mind when he called together pastors and artists to Austin for the magnificent symposium "Transforming Culture." Face-to-face, ear-to-ear, heart-to-heart, these individuals acknowledged their need for each other and discovered fresh ways to connect and integrate.

I know how transformative this was. I was there at the amazing event orchestrated by David Taylor and Larry Linen-schmidt. I've attended scores of conferences for writers and artists. I've been involved in many gatherings for Christian leaders and ministers. But I have seldom seen such an enlivening spirit (Holy Spirit) at work to initiate new partnerships. Symbiosis? Yes! As celebratory as a wedding!

I first knew David Taylor as an undomesticated student at Regent College, stirring up his profs and fellow students with tempestuous ideas and questions. I remember him rushing impetuously into chapel on Tuesdays, sprinting down the auditorium stairs two at a time to make an announcement, red mane flying, seemingly on fire. At the time I thought, *This guy is either a maniac or a young prophet.* His enthusiasm for God and for the arts was intense and appealing, and I thought, *All he needs is time!*

And in the grace of God David has put in the time, grown in influence, and committed himself to the care and feeding of the whole church as well as of promising artists (one of whom he married!). I've witnessed firsthand his deft and exuberant work as Arts Pastor of Hope Chapel in Austin, and have wished for that energy to be contagious across the continent.

In his introduction to this book, David presents a metaphor of the pastor as gardener, a theme that has invigorated my own writing. I'm an enthusiastic tiller of soil, one who cultivates and guards the plants in my yard (maybe *garden* derives from the idea of a guardian?). Another metaphor, this time from Joshua Banner, one of this collection's contributors, is closely related: pastor as farmer. I love these ways of envisioning the task of the pastor. (The words *pastor* and *pastoral* reflect their origin in the word for *shepherd*—one who cares for a flock, leading, feeding, sheltering, sometimes rescuing.) Metaphors can bring theology to life, pinning down abstract ideas into vivid pictures that we can comprehend by way of imagination.

Another metaphor for artful beauty as an exhibition of God's grace keeps visiting my imagination—a reservoir of mountain spring water brimming with marine life. It is glorious. The sun glints from its surface. The wind excites it into ripples. It reflects the blue and white, or thundery gray, of the sky. It is a mirror for the sun and moon. For years it has been building, dammed up, waiting for release, impatient for its generosity to be poured into the valley below with its fields of wheat, its orchards, its forests. Though a narrow spillway has allowed a trickle of life and health to reach the valley, for some valley-dwellers the reservoir has been seen as dangerous, fearful, a symbol of potential flood that could destroy life. Better to keep this bounty under control behind the barrier of rock and concrete. Better not to allow it to pour too freely. Better to narrow its course into the well-worn channels permitted by tradition or custom.

But in the church a surge is happening in response to human thirst! Living water is beginning to gush! Let's welcome the overflowing torrent! Mixed metaphors? Okay. But our God is the God of plenty, who uses multiple word pictures throughout Scripture to illuminate the minds of both writers and readers.

So, welcome pastors! Welcome artists! Be enriched and encouraged as you read the words in this book, sharing its vitality with others in your communities of faith. As you spread the word like water in the desert, I'm trusting that God's generosity and glory will spring up in you like good fruit. May it inhabit you, illumine you, join you with each other in an outpouring of divine beauty.

Luci Shaw
Bellingham, Washington

Acknowledgments

Heartfelt gratitude goes first to the seven writers who agreed to throw their weight behind this project: Joshua Banner, Jeremy Begbie, Andy Crouch, Barbara Nicolosi, Eugene Peterson, Lauren Winner, and John Witvliet. I'm keenly grateful for the ways each of them has spoken into my life. I owe special gratitude to Bob Hosack, acquisitions editor at Baker Books, for believing in me from the beginning. I had met Bob long ago at Regent College. While sitting for coffee one day, he asked if I had any book ideas, to which I said yes, but regrettably only ideas. Ten years later we now have ideas *and* a book. But this book would be thick and unwieldy if it weren't for the sharp eye of Robert Hand. Robert has been an invaluable ally in this venture.

I wish to acknowledge an intellectual debt I owe to many of my professors at Regent College: J. I. Packer, Gordon Fee, James Houston, Eugene Peterson, Bruce Waltke, Thena Ayres, Paul Stevens, Rikki Watts, Craig Gay, Miriam Adeney, Loren Wilkinson, and Maxine Hancock. They not only inspired me with a vision for a Great Tradition Christian faith, but also willingly indulged my requests to spin every paper toward the arts.

I must certainly thank Larry Linenschmidt for his partnership with me on the symposium. His Texas jokes kept me in good humor throughout. The symposium would not have happened without his encouragement. Thanks to Bob Fullilove for transcribing Nicolosi's talk. Thanks also to First Evangelical Free Church and to the many people who volunteered to make the symposium a great success.

Many thanks go to the fabulous friends who took time to read sections of this book: Adam Langley, Kate Van Dyke, John Wilson, Kelly Foster, Ann Cogdell, Ahna Phillips, and Susanna Banner. Also sincere thanks to Jason Byassee, Jeremy Begbie, and Travis Hines. I am especially grateful to the artists who contributed their work to this book: Katherine Brimberry, Andy Davis, Shaun Fox, Baker Galloway, Anita Horton, Jim Janknegt, Laura Jennings, Phaedra Taylor, Rick Van Dyke, Samantha Wedelich.

I want to offer wholehearted gratitude to the dear people at Hope Chapel. They took a risk in hiring me as their first "arts pastor" and they watched me grow up into the man and pastor I've become. A particular thanks to Ron Parrish, Jack and Debbie Dorman, Dan Davis, Geno Hildebrandt, Debbie Bjork (my first TA), the intrepid members of the Arts Council, the cadre of intercessors who supported me with many prayers (especially John and Kareen), the staff, the congregation and all the superbly gifted artists who came and went through the doors of Hope Chapel looking for a home.

Deep appreciation goes to two friends who have taught me to love well and to live well: Mike Akel and Jeffrey Travis.

I love my family immensely: Cliff, Christine, Brendan, Cormac, Skye, and Bronwyn Warner; Scranton, Stephanie, Speight, and Sohren Twohey; and, with the greatest affection for supporting me with such generous and sacrificial love from the beginning, my parents, Bill and Yvonne Taylor.

Lastly, I thank my beloved wife, Phaedra Jean Taylor. She has endured, with a fierce grace, my blustery moods, quixotic visions, animated speeches, mumblings to myself, hair styles, and my strange desire to live a "stable but very exciting life." I honor her with this book.

Jim Janknegt, "Annunciation." Oil on canvas.

Introduction

A case could be made that, ever since the early nineteenth century, if not before, much of the finest art and music of spiritual and theological import—whether popular or highly cultivated—has been created without the Church's blessing or, indeed, the Church's knowledge.

Frank Burch Brown, *Good Taste,*
Bad Taste, and Christian Taste

When *Time* magazine compiled a list of the one hundred most significant people in twentieth-century art and entertainment there were only five who had shown any public signs of Christian faith.

Steve Turner, *Imagine: A Vision*
for Christians in the Arts

A parishioner and artist friend came up to me one Sunday and said, "You are not a pastor." It was a strange thing to hear as I stood near the pulpit at the end of a service. At the time, I had been a pastor for six years, specifically the "arts pastor." *Of course I'm a pastor*, I thought. *That's nonsense.*

In my mind I summoned a litany of my accomplishments, both to defend myself and to put him in his place. I had sat for hours in my office listening to artists pouring out their hearts. I had run a three-week arts festival that would extend the mission of our church into the liveliest parts of the city. I had established an artist-in-residence program. I had directed the Ragamuffin Film Festival, about which Austin's arts and entertainment weekly, *The Chronicle*, remarked, "It's culture-jamming operating under a higher state of grace." I wanted to say, "You *see* all that I've done on your behalf to help you, an artist, find a home in the church? What do you mean I'm not a pastor?"

Even as I mentally rehearsed the list of deeds, I knew what he was really trying to say. He meant: "You are not a good pastor. You are doing many good things with the arts, yes. Yet you are failing to actually *shepherd* us, to *lead* us." I knew that my friend deeply cared for me, which was why he risked upsetting me. Later in the week as I walked through my neighborhood processing his statement, I could hear myself saying, a little resentfully, "I'm doing my best. What more do you want?"

A thought that continually sits at the margins of my consciousness drifted toward me again that Sunday morning: *I really do not know what I am doing. This work of art and the church is too much for me. I do not know to what end I am working. And I do not know if any of my efforts will remain.*

The Problem

I worked as a pastor of an arts ministry at a church in Austin, Texas, for twelve years.[1] These were twelve of the most fulfilling years of my life. The leadership endowed me with a blank check to try almost anything, and the trust they placed in my young hands still boggles my mind. Yet with a team of brave friends, try almost anything I did. We instituted five art exhibits that rotated throughout the year in response to the church calendar. We got artists into small groups. We got them reading books by Dutch Reformed philosopher Calvin Seerveld and Jewish novelist Chaim Potok. We got the congregation one Sunday to move their bodies *en masse* under the direction of professional modern dancers—a truly

18

terrifying experience for the many introverts in that room. On one occasion we hung a thousand beeswax-soaked paper butterflies over the entire span of the sanctuary. This was an art installation that sought to remind us of Jesus's words in Matthew 5:45, that grace falls from heaven on the righteous and unrighteous alike. Artists who had been hurt by the church returned home. Singer–songwriters bravely ventured into the city to play the coffeeshop circuit. Two of our filmmakers signed contracts with Universal Studios.

During these years God awakened a tremendous amount of energy in our community. We saw him transform lives, spiritually and relationally. Many made peace with the fact that God had called them as artists, and there was no need to be ashamed any more. There was very little we did not attempt at least once during those years, succeeding at some and failing at others, always grateful for the chance to explore freely under the covering of the leadership.

Yet while we accomplished plenty, I know now that I struggled against the debilitating effects of two forces.

The first force is a variant of pragmatism. In this view, experiences supremely govern our perception of what is good or bad. If an activity produces a positive experience, then it must be good. In the spring of 2002, for example, I replaced the sermon with a fifty-minute play on the life of Adam and Eve. The congregation responded enthusiastically, amazed at how theater could communicate, in its own vernacular and allusive language, the Word of God. So we kept doing things like it. If the outcome is unsuccessful, however—that is, if the majority responds negatively—then it must be bad. For instance, I once introduced a contemplative musical experience into the Sunday service. In the aftermath I had some members complain that our church was becoming "Catholic." From then on we restricted all "liturgical" elements to our monthly, all-voluntary Compline service.

Experience, alongside Scripture, is an important source for our understanding of the Christian life. The 120 believers of

Acts 2 would surely bear witness to this. But what happened to me as a pastor is that I assessed my work too heavily according to whether an artistic activity produced a positive or negative experience apart from any *theological* consideration. Very few of our conversations as artists revolved around a theological understanding of the church—or of worship—or of art—or of what it means to be human—and therefore of how we ought to see art properly serving the church, apart from whether an experience felt good or bad.

Eventually I burned out on artistic activities that worked. I needed a bigger reason than successful experiences to be doing art in the church.

The second force is a confusion about art in my ecclesial tradition. My tradition is "mutt Protestant." As a child I was raised in a fundamentalist missionary subculture in Guatemala.[2] During my college years I attended Lutheran, Episcopalian, Vineyard, and Bible churches. In seminary I became Anglican. As a pastor at Hope Chapel I worked in a midsized nondenominational charismatic church.

My particular Protestant tradition offers few artistic resources to the church. Music and oratory will be the exception, maybe also the literary arts, though only in a few pockets of history. To be sure, there are many fine exceptions to the general statement I am about to make—such as the Methodists who built a magnificent neogothic cathedral on the campus of Duke University[3] or a Christian Reformed Church in Seattle that recently patronized an art show by the Vancouver Project.[4] Still, it is typical of most Protestant experiences of art that the ear trumps the eye. The intellect and emotion trump the body. Activity trumps contemplation. And a minimalist rather than maximalist aesthetic will usually be seen as more representative of the "pure gospel." One church will exhibit keen support of stained glass windows, yet react less than thoughtfully to the inclusion of film into worship. Another church will produce first-class theater, yet impulsively dismiss hymns as stuffy.

As a working pastor I found my tradition ambivalent, if not actively resistant, to the artistic life—to the imagination, the emotions, the senses, the material realm, and beauty. Eventually this too wore me down. If I were a gardener, I would say that my tradition offered me thin soil with little hope for a flourishing of the arts. At worst it taught me to view the arts as ultimately expendable, a luxury far from the center of biblical Christianity.

What is my point? It is this: as a pastor I evaluated my work only by its pragmatic effects, and I traveled haphazardly through my ecclesial tradition because I lacked a larger vision for art and the church. I could not shepherd well the artists under my care because I had no final vision for where I should lead them.

Protestantism—in my case evangelical Protestantism—handed me neither a big picture (a theology) nor a sense of how art and the church could hold together (a tradition). What I was left with were strategies and programs, and fairly good ones. But they failed to pull me, my artist friends, our congregation, and our brothers and sisters throughout the city and the world into something bigger than ourselves.[5] Many of us, in fact, have felt the lack of a comprehensive, systematic, integrating, and grounding vision.

The Aim of This Book

This book aims to redress this deficiency. It aims to inspire the church, in its life and mission, with an expansive vision for the arts. By "the arts" I mean at least music, dance, drama, poetry and other literary arts, visual arts, film, and architecture. This book seeks to show how the many parts of the landscape of church and art can hold together.

Few books have been printed in this vein. If we walked into a bookstore (real or virtual), we'd probably find three kinds of volumes on art and Christianity. We would find books on art and worship, from Horton Davies's magisterial *Worship* and *Theology in England* to Dan Kimball's *Emerging Worship: Creating Worship Gatherings for New Generations.* We would find books that offer a Christian perspective on a specific medium, such as Robert Johnston's *Reel Spirituality* or Betty Spackman's *A Profound Weakness: Christians and Kitsch.* And we'd come across general reflections on art and Christian life. Madeleine L'Engle's *Walking on Water* represents a first-rate example of this type.

But not many books offer a complex reflection on the arts and the church—the church, that is, as the gathered community in its local manifestation and in its varied functions, such as worship, discipleship, community, service, and mission.

For whom is this book written? It is written for pastors and artists along with lay leaders working in the context of the church. This book is for pastors who gather in cathedrals or in junior high cafeterias, for artists in the urban core or, as the case may be, out in the cornfields. It aims to inform our ecclesiology as Protestant Christians, regardless of our material or missional particulars.

My hope is that this book will also be of benefit to educators and seminary students, to critical observers of Christianity and the arts, and to all those who seek a common vocabulary to advance the discussion of the church's mission of artmaking.

The Historical Occasion for the Book

A conference that took place in April 2008 in Austin, Texas, "Transforming Culture: A Vision for the Church and the Arts," gave rise to this book.[6] The conference brought together pastors and artists to explore the church's relationship to art. Almost eight hundred people, from the Netherlands to North Dakota, descended on the campus of First Evangelical Free Church for three days of energizing conversation and delightful table fellowship. The conference opened with a modern dance piece and closed with a poem titled "Psalm 151," an encomium to

22

God's creative workmanship. All throughout it featured the work of printmakers, folk singers, actors, filmmakers, and other creatives who gave sensible expression to the ideas of the conference. We worshiped together. We prayed together. Pastors and artists found themselves really listening to each other—sometimes agreeing, sometimes strongly disagreeing, but always graciously—and what a joy that was to witness.

The seminars included topics such as "Visual Homiletics: How to Preach to the Eye as Well as to the Ear" and "Seminaries and the Aesthetic Formation of Pastors." A favorite was the epic title John Wilson, editor of *Books & Culture*, drummed up: "The Contemporary Culture of Books, Literature, and Ideas: Or, What the Heck People Are Writing about These Days and How All These Ideas Are Shaping the Imagination of Christians, Consciously or Unconsciously, Immediately or Eventually . . . and Why This Matters to Churches."

The conference considered six questions that turned on a single vision: a vision of the church and the arts that is theologically informed, biblically grounded, liturgically sensitive, artistically alive, and missionally shrewd. After the conference I recruited two more writers for this book: Lauren Winner and Joshua Banner. They, along with the original six speakers from the conference (pastors and artists themselves), give voice to what I hope is a coherent vision.

The book begins at the beginning: "The Gospel." It ends with a vision of the church's future in the year 2058: "The Future." In between, the book addresses key components for an integrated vision: "The Worshiper," "The Art Patron," "The Pastor," "The Artist," "The Practitioner," and "The Dangers."

A Summary of the Book

In chapter 1, Andy Crouch grounds all our artmaking in the fundamental category of culture making. If we can conclude, in particular from Genesis, that culture making is good, then we can also conclude that our artmaking is good. All art is a gift, he argues, not an achievement. Like the entire gospel, art establishes its purpose not in its utility but in something bigger than itself: grace. And like worship, it pulls us into something bigger than ourselves, pulling all our play and all our pain into the beautiful life of God in Christ.

Following this, John Witvliet takes us directly to the arena of worship. He asks, How can art serve to deepen and challenge our corporate worship? He identifies three tendencies that concern him in churches today. One is the tendency to allow our artistic activity to become predominantly about the individual and what he or she wants. The second is to let our artistic work remain easy for the congregation—"melodies, images, metaphors, rhythms, and palettes of color that succeed at making worship pleasant and utterly innocuous." The third is to allow our art to slip into rote or even idolatrous ways of worshiping God. Witvliet offers three hearty antidotes to these tendencies in a way that dovetails nicely with the later chapter on dangers.

Next, Lauren Winner takes the position of the worshiper in the pew. She becomes for this book the everywoman. Winner explores not only her own reasons for loving, needing, and being irrevocably shaped by art but also why she believes the church, perhaps to our surprise, often does care about art. An idea she examines in depth is the Jewish principle of *hiddur mitzvah*, "the idea that one does not just do the commandments, one 'beautifies' them." In doing so she helps us see aspects of Scripture and Christian life with fresh eyes.

This is exactly what Eugene Peterson testifies in his chapter that artists have done for him. He wonders why he's been plunked into this book about artists. "I'm a pastor," he says, "and a pretty conventional pastor at that." Happily for the rest of us pastors, he voices a widespread concern: What do I as a pastor have to do with art? He says, simply, "I'm here to be a witness. I am here to give witness to the decisive and critical influence that artists have had in my life as a pastor

24

in a Christian church." Then he goes on to talk about Willi Ossa (a painter), Gerry Baxter (an architect), and Judith (a textile artist)—that is to say, folks you might find in your own congregation.

These are the kinds of artists Barbara Nicolosi encounters regularly in Hollywood, California. In her essay Nicolosi recounts her experience as a minister to artists on the verge of losing their sanity. Instead of allowing them to self-indulge, however, she calls them into something bigger than themselves: the realm of beauty. If we get beauty right, we will get the pastoring of artists right because that is their terrain. Their terrain, she insists, is not propaganda or boosting people's self-esteem. Barbara's overriding goal is to help us recognize who the artists in our communities are so we can shepherd them well. Her words are not easy; they're spicy. But we need them.

In chapter 6, Joshua Banner takes us to a street-level version of our discussion. Having worked in a church as a pastor to artists, he has a good sense of what works and what doesn't. He reminds us pastors that it's not so much about technique as a right understanding of our role. Our role, he maintains, is that of a farmer. As farmers we won't get everything right, but we will know that our main job is to pay careful attention to people's lives. With that framework in place, Joshua goes on to talk about three aspects of his work with artists: pastoring, promoting, and producing. And he does so with the gentle, confident hand of an experienced farmer-pastor.

In the chapter that follows, I (David Taylor) remain in the practical arena and identify some of the dangers we might encounter. What are possible excesses and misuses of art? How might art undermine the calling of the church? I identify six specific dangers: bad art, art as a supersaturating agent, the inordinate love of an art form, the utilitarian reduction of art, art as a form of distraction, and immature behavior. I also suggest three qualities of healthy artistic growth. The question, I propose, is not "Will we continue to use art?"

but rather "How can we grow well in our continuing use of art?" I propose that our artistic growth should be relationally ordered, contextually relative, and organically rhythmed.

From hazards we turn finally to hope. Jeremy Begbie notes the temptation of Christians when speaking about the future is to play the role of the futurologist. We look around at life in the present, then forecast forward. This leads either to resignation ("put up with what we've got and wait for heaven") or triumphalism ("we can create heaven-on-earth now"). But the New Testament invites us to move from God's promised future (the final vision of Revelation) to a vision of what can happen in the present by the power of the Spirit. Jeremy names six ways in which the Spirit can erupt into our present with good news for the arts and our churches over the next half century.

One Last Note

The authors of this book come from different traditions—Anglican and Presbyterian, charismatic and Catholic. We do not agree on everything. Our voices are distinct, as you will soon learn. We certainly do not presume to have this subject figured out. Yet we share a great deal of respect for each other and our earnest desire is to encourage fellow travelers in this common work. To this end, each author has recommended five books. Many of these will be great to read with others. Our hope is that these resources will motivate readers to keep asking good questions.

In a piece Jeremy Begbie wrote for a fine collection of essays on beauty, *The Beauty of God*, he articulates a vision for the artist. I believe his vision is apropos to this book. In it he sees the artist as

> physical and embodied, set in the midst of a God-given world vibrant with a dynamic beauty of its own, not simply "there" like a brute fact to be escaped or violently abused but there as a gift from a God of overflowing beauty, a gift for us to interact

with vigorously, shape and reshape, form and transform, and in this way fashion something as consistent and dazzlingly novel as [Johann Sebastian Bach's] *Goldberg Variations,* art that can anticipate the beauty previewed and promised in Jesus Christ.[7]

It is within such an "overflowing beauty" that this book seeks to find its place. The title, *For the Beauty of the Church,* is a play on the old hymn, "For the Beauty of the Earth" (1864), and the terms are intentionally chosen. It is my desire that all our artistic actions on behalf of the church lead to the fuller beauty of the church, a beauty that derives from God and pulls us into the boundless and everlasting beauty of God. Perhaps our artistic actions in the years to come will even redress the sad state Frank Burch Brown and Steve Turner identify in the opening quotations of this introduction. My prayer is that these essays will prod us to clearer thinking and to shrewder action. My prayer is that, by the grace of Christ and under the Spirit's supervision, they will stir us together to develop a theology capable of sustaining a long-lasting, fruit-bearing tradition of artmaking by the church, for the church, for the glory of God in the church, and for the good of the world. A great company of men and women across the world yearn and sweat toward this vision.

In the third verse of the above hymn, songwriter Folliot Pierpoint declaims:

> For the joy of ear and eye,
> for the heart and mind's delight,
> for the mystic harmony,
> linking sense to sound and sight;
> Lord of all, to thee we raise
> this our hymn of grateful praise.

For all the ways in which the arts can not only delight our senses but enable us to fulfill God's mission on earth—for this indeed we raise our hymn of grateful praise.

Katherine Brimberry, "Adam's Malady." Photo-polymer gravure.

The Gospel

*How Is Art a Gift, a Calling,
and an Obedience?*

ANDY CROUCH

One of the great good things about the Christian liturgical year is its rhythm of fasting and feasting, and one of the great good things about the English language is how close those two words are to one another in spelling and sound. The two words seem to come from entirely different sources—*fast* from Norse, *feast* from Old French—but they have ended up as linguistic neighbors, cousins if not siblings. A slight change of vowel, the addition of a written *e*, and we move from one pole of human experience to the other—from want to abundance—held together by the fact that both of these are deliberate words. You can go hungry, through no fault of your own, from famine; you can overeat without really meaning to, as any kid who has finished a serving of cotton candy can attest. But both fasting and feasting require commitment, preparation, and attention.

A conference on the church and the arts, or a book on the same topic, is likewise not something you stumble into unprepared. For three glorious spring days in Austin, Texas, two weeks after a brisk late-March Easter, pastors, artists, patrons, writers, dancers, and musicians came together deliberately, with every intention of preparing, serving, and enjoying a feast. I ended up thinking about this conference, especially the talks that gave it structure, as a multicourse meal at the chef's table. When you sit at the chef's table in a fine restaurant, it is customary not to order from the menu, but simply to ask the chef to prepare and serve whatever she or he likes—whatever she or he loves—and enjoy the proximity and intimacy, along with the bustle and noise, of being close to the action, close to people who have trained and honed their skills and their senses in the interests of offering something exceptional. People who have learned to prepare feasts.

I saw my own role in this three-day feast not so much as trying to offer a main course, but perhaps more like the waiter who seats guests at the table and offers a preview of what may be coming out of the kitchen. Another customary element of the chef's table is the *amuse-bouche* or *amuse-gueule*, the surprising little tasty snack brought out before the first course is even served. It is designed to whet your appetite, remind you why you came, and awaken your senses and your mind, preparing you for the amazing food that is to come.

And so I offer this chapter in the spirit of the *amuse-bouche*. I hope to convince you that the gospel is more truly and deeply about culture in general, and the arts in particular, than we have yet imagined. I offered to the friends in Austin, and offer to you now, a few small, bite-sized observations that could provoke us, awaken us, and make us ready to talk with one another.

In the day that the Lord God made the earth and the heavens, when no plant of the field was yet in the earth and no herb of the field had yet sprung up—for the Lord God had not caused it to rain upon the earth, and there was no one to till the ground; but a stream would rise from the earth, and water the whole face of the ground—then the Lord God formed man from the dust of the ground, and breathed into his nostrils the breath of life; and the man became a living being.

And the Lord God planted a garden in Eden, in the east; and there he put the man whom he had formed. Out of the ground the Lord God made to grow every tree that is pleasant to the sight and good for food, the tree of life also in the midst of the garden, and the tree of the knowledge of good and evil. A river flows out of Eden to water the garden, and from there it divides and becomes four branches. The name of the first is Pishon; it is the one that flows around the whole land of Havilah, where there is gold; and the gold of that land is good; bdellium and onyx stone are there. The name of the second river is Gihon; it is the one that flows around the whole land of Cush. The name of the third river is Tigris, which flows east of Assyria. And the fourth river is the Euphrates. The Lord God took the man and put him in the garden of Eden to till it and keep it. (Gen. 2:4–15)

The best definition I have found for culture comes from the Christian cultural critic Ken Myers, and I summarize his definition this way: culture is *what we make of the world, in both senses.*

Culture is the stuff we make of the world. And it is the sense we make of the world. Culture is material, and culture is meaningful. And the two go together. The way we make sense is by making stuff. The way we find our way to meaning is to make something new. Culture is meaning-making. But it is always also blessedly material. The common image of culture as being like the water that a fish swims in is misleading if it implies that culture is an imperceptible, immaterial environment. Culture is made of the raw material of creation.

It is commonly said that culture is a distinctively human activity. This is what human beings do: we make something of the world, in the dual sense of new cultural goods and new, culturally mediated interpretations of the world.

But this story from Genesis offers a surprising twist on that commonplace assumption. For Genesis 2 presents the Lord God himself as a culture maker—a cultivator making something of the world. Unlike Genesis 1, Genesis 2 is not about *creatio ex nihilo*—or more precisely, creation out of the sheer uncreated love and being of the divine Society. It is about *creatio ex creatis*—creation out of what was created. Making something of the world. "The Lord God formed Adam from the dust of the earth." And even more striking: "The Lord God planted a garden in Eden, in the east." A garden is not just nature. A garden is nature plus culture. The first gardener—the first one to plant, to water, to select, protect, weed, and nurture—is not Adam. It is God.

Culture is God's gift to Adam. Without culture, without a garden, how could this human dustling survive in the wildness of even a very good created world? God does not just give Adam free rein in the trackless world. God plants a garden. God begins the work of culture before he gives the work to Adam. Culture is God's creation as much as nature is. The Lord God's hands have dug into the dirt. He has touched it. He has blessed it. Everything Adam does as a gardener will begin with what God did. Culture is God's idea.

A second observation from this amazing *amuse-bouche* of an introductory story, this table-setting tale from the author of Torah: "Out of the ground the Lord God made to grow every tree that is pleasant to the sight and good for food" (v. 9). This garden, this original gift of culture, is not just a utilitarian source of nourishment. It is not just a vegetable garden, populated with a healthful array of plants that will provide the Creator's RDA of nutrients to the dutiful fruit- and vegetable-eating human gardener. It is also a place of beauty. The trees of the garden are not just good *for* something. They are good simply in the beholding. They are beautiful.

But even more striking than the description of the vegetation is the least remarked-upon part of the whole story in Genesis 2. "The name of the first [river] is Pishon; it is the one that flows around the whole land of Havilah, where there is gold; and the gold of that land is good; bdellium and onyx stone are there" (v. 12).

Why does the author indulge in this metallurgical excursion—with its digression within an excursion, "And the gold of that land is good"? Is this a treasure map for future readers? What is the point of this list of precious natural resources? Note that these are not primarily *useful* minerals or substances. The text does not say that the land of Havilah has good iron, granite, and bauxite. These are substances whose only real value is in their beauty. God has located the garden in a place where the natural explorations of its human cultivators will bring them into contact with substances that will invite the creation of beauty.

I owe to Makoto Fujimura the further observation that these substances are hidden. They are not like the low-hanging fruit of the garden's trees. They are latent—lying below the surface of the very good world. Only by exploration and excavation will they be discovered. Only by experimentation and craftsmanship will their possibilities be disclosed. God has placed primordial humanity in a world that will only reach its full potential for beauty when it is cultivated, explored—where more goodness waits to be unearthed. The world is even better than it appears. The gold of that land is good.

A third and darker, sadder theme: there is exploration, and there is exploitation. In the garden is one tree that, like the others, is explicitly said to be "good for food, and a delight to the eyes"—nutritious and beautiful like the rest. But it is also "to be desired to make one wise" (Gen. 3:6).

Or so the woman thinks, and so the serpent implies. It is a means to an extrinsic end—and a very implausible end at that. How likely is it that a fruit could make you wise? That is not what God had said—God simply said that it was the tree of the knowledge of good and evil. But simply to know good and evil is not to be wise, much less to be "like God," as the serpent so craftily insinuates. To be wise is not only to know good and evil but to be able to choose good and resist evil. Nothing in that fruit would make that kind of wisdom possible.

And here is where human beings try to make something of the world that the world simply cannot yield. Here is where culture oversteps its boundaries. The man and the woman try to use the world for something more than it could ever be—to replace relationship with God, relationship with the only true source of wisdom, with a created thing. It is not enough for the world to be beautiful and good—we want it to be self-sufficient. We want to be self-sufficient within it. No more waiting for the Lord God to walk in the garden in the cool of the day, no more lengthy process of maturation and education in the way of wisdom. The man and the woman take and eat, and set in motion the process by which everything that God had originally given as a gift, a sign of relationship and dependence, will be twisted into a right, something grasped from a world presumed to be threatened and threatening, something that insulates us from needing relationship or dependence.

And what is the first thing that happens after the man and woman have eaten? Culture. "They sewed fig leaves together and made loincloths for themselves" (Gen. 3:7). They make something of the world to ward off their sudden exposure to one another and to God. Culture is no longer the good, gracious activity of tending a good, gracious world. It is a defensive measure, an instrumental use of the world to ward off the world's greatest threat—the threat, suddenly a threat, of being known, of trusting one's fellow creatures and one's Creator. The fig leaves are useful—barely—but they are not a delight to the eyes. They are strictly instrumental, hastily assembled to solve a problem and secure a measure of protection. They are torn from the living, good garden and stitched into a rudimentary, fading, dying, withering form of protection from—from what? Not even protection from the world, which has not yet, at this moment in the story, fallen under the curse. Just protection from one another, bone of bone and flesh of flesh. And protection from the one who had breathed life into dust.

This is what human beings will make of the world in the sad downward spiral of Genesis 3 through 11: more and more effective forms of protection from any sense of dependence. Cain's cultivated field will become a murder scene. Lamech, the father of herdsmen and musicians and toolmakers, will murder again. Noah will plant a vineyard and become the first binge drinker. In Genesis 11, culture will reach its apex and its nadir at the same time. The exploration and excavation yield not gold, bdellium, and onyx, but brick and bitumen, clay and asphalt, the dull and useful stuff of tower building, useful for building ourselves "a city, and a tower with its top in the heavens, and a name for ourselves, lest we be scattered abroad upon the face of the whole earth" (Gen. 11:4). *Ourselves, us, ourselves, us.* We will steal back enough of the world from its Maker to be able to eke out life ourselves, self-naming, self-contained.

But one fourth and final observation can be snatched from the grim story that follows Genesis 3. There are fig leaves, but at the moment of expulsion from the garden there are also leather garments. There is murder, but there is also a mark of mercy. There is wickedness, but there is also an ark, and a covenant, and a rainbow. Far from washing his hands of the dirty, dusty business of culture, abandoning it to human beings at their best and worst, the Creator continues to create *ex creatis*. He stays in the story. Indeed, he ultimately enters the story at the point of greatest pressure and pain. And on the night before he suffers the worst that wayward human culture can do, this is what he does: he takes bread and wine into his hands, lifts them up, and blesses them. Bread and wine, not wheat and grapes. Bread and wine are culture, not just nature. They are good for food and a delight to the eyes. Jesus takes culture, blesses it, breaks it, and gives it to his friends. Taken, broken, blessed, and given, these cultural goods, these "creatures of bread and wine" as the old prayer book had it, become sign and presence of God in the world.

What does all this mean for art, and for the question I have been given to answer: "How is art a gift, a calling, and an obedience?"

I think this question can only be answered in the context of a larger question: "How is *culture* a gift, a calling, and an obedience?" Do we believe that culture is a gift? Do we believe that culture is a calling and an obedience? Or is culture a distraction, a detour, a dead end? Do we believe that culture can be taken, blessed, broken, and given? Is culture a gift?

Art sharpens and focuses these questions in a unique way. And it is precisely because Christians of a certain kind have been so uncertain on the answer to these broader questions about culture that they have been so uncertain in their attitude toward art. Put another way, our response to art, the way we talk or do not talk about art, the way we make or avoid making art, is the truest diagnostic test of our underlying, perhaps implicit and unexplored, beliefs about culture.

Why is this so? I would suggest that it is so because art can be provisionally defined as those aspects of culture that cannot be reduced to utility.

Art is, perhaps, one way of naming everything we as cultural beings do that cannot be explained in terms of its usefulness. It is not the realm of the useless exactly, but the incapable-of-being-expressed-as-useful. That which cannot be turned into a means to an end, but asserts itself as an end—intrinsically, and in some senses inexplicably, worthwhile.

What is the point of a painting? What is the use of a song? What is the purpose of a poem? Or, to make the point more finely, why have wallpaper when wallboard would do? Why craft a careful sentence when a stolid and stupid one would do just as well? Why buy a thin laptop when you could buy a thick one for less money? In each of these latter examples, we are singling out the artful quality in a cultural good, and it cannot be explained in the same way that we can explain the other qualities of that good. We can explain why we would want a wall, but why do we want wallpaper? Can we explain it in any terms other than itself?

This leads to another related feature of what we call art. Artful goods are stubbornly themselves. They resist transmutation into something else. They cannot be translated without loss. You can translate the words of a technical manual from one language to another with no significant loss in content or context. (Based on the manuals for electronic goods that arrive on our shores, we must admit that this does not always happen—but it is possible!) But you cannot translate a poem. The best you can do is offer another poem in another language that echoes and responds to the original poem. You cannot even paraphrase a poem in its own language—poetry resists paraphrase. The only words that can be used are the original words.

You can take a photograph of a painting, but no matter how high its resolution and technical quality, the photograph fails to capture much about the original painting that can only be known in its presence. For a few years in high school I worked in a structural steel company as the blueprint boy. I took architectural drawings on sepia paper, ran them through a machine that reeked of ammonia, exposed and fixed their images onto blueprints, and sent off the blueprints. If I did my job well, there was nothing lost in the transmission of the information from original to copy. The copy was just as useful as the original. That is not true of art. And it wasn't even entirely true of the blueprints, for the original drawings had the imprint of the drafter's hand, the even, careful lines of his 0.7-millimeter pencil, the traces of his gum eraser. There was something beautiful and artful about draftsmanship that was only present in a residual, ghostly way in the blueprint. All the information, all the use, could be perfectly transmitted. The artfulness could not.

I think that we Christians have made our peace, more or less, with useful culture. Especially when it can be used as a means for our own ends. If the song has Christian lyrics, if the painting has an appropriately pious subject, if the technology is used to deliver the gospel—which is often itself conceived rather like a blueprint, a technical drawing explaining the mechanics of salvation—we are ready and even eager to be culture makers. Contemporary churches are full of more or less artful delivery mechanisms for (no doubt important) messages.

And we should acknowledge that for a long stretch of Christian history, including some of our finest moments as creators of culture, an overwhelming majority of that which was made with conscious artistic intention did indeed serve explicitly Christian purposes. Icons, cathedrals, frescoes, illuminated manuscripts—all these were beautifully and specifically Christian in their subject. But even the artists who made these goods couldn't help but explore beyond the boundaries of strictly religious usefulness, and in this way they went far beyond the straightforward purposefulness of so much art created for the church today. There were stained-glass windows, but there were also gargoyles. In the margins of the manuscripts frolicked deer and birds. There were extra characters in the paintings, not mentioned in the original story, each of whom had their own specific gravity, their own being, their own value. The stretches of music untethered to lyrics grew longer and more wonderfully complex. There was too much good in the world to be constrained within the bounds of religious utility.

And this is exactly as it should be. For what is Christian faith itself but the embodied conviction that religion is not, after all, about utility? For many of our ancestors and many of our contemporaries, religion was and is a means to an end.

It is a way to cajole the gods into propitious attitudes, to bend the mysterious forces of the cosmos a little bit toward our needs by the right mixture of supplication and praise. But what if the world, from beginning to end, is a gift? What if God is more utterly, completely for us than we could ever be for ourselves? What if we no longer have to offer a sacrifice that might waft up into his nostrils and compel his distracted attention—what if he himself has taken the initiative, become the sacrifice, torn the temple veil? What is left but gloriously unuseful prayer and praise?

What we do in our churches, when we do what we should be doing, is unuseful! It is better than useful. The economy of grace overflows with the unuseful. Does prayer work? Should prayer work? No. Prayer does not work. It does something better than work. Prayer brings us into the life of the one by whom all things were made and are being remade. It aligns our life with the one who suffered most deeply on behalf of all that is broken in the world, and through whose sufferings the world has been saved, is being saved, and will be saved.

So we Christians have a lot at stake in the unuseful. We stake our worship every Sunday on the belief that we do not need to convince God to be useful to us, and he does not require us to be useful to him. At the height of Israel's sacrificial system, he tells them: "For every wild animal of the forest is mine, the cattle on a thousand hills. . . . If I were hungry, I would not tell you, for the world and all that is in it is mine" (Ps. 50:10, 12). We know what it is like to invest our energies in something that repudiates the world's whole idea of utility. Worship is obedience, but not the kind of obedience that placates a vengeful master. Worship is a calling, but not the kind of calling that carries the threat of displeasure should it be carried out inadequately or imperfectly. The best word for worship—the best word for the Christian life that is summed up by and sustained by worship—is that it is a *gift*.

This is why I snuck a sneaky little academic word in earlier when I said that art can be *provisionally* defined as those aspects of culture that cannot be reduced to utility. Actually that definition is not quite complete, because it is also true of worship. Art and worship stand together on the common ground of the unuseful. And this is why our attitude toward art ultimately has a great deal to do with our attitude toward worship. Much is at stake in whether we think that our worship is a free response to grace or an exercise in persuasion, an effort to get either God or people to do what we want them to do. If we have a utilitarian attitude toward art, if we require it to justify itself in terms of its usefulness to our ends, it is very likely that we will end up with the same attitude toward worship, and ultimately toward God.

Let me expand on this a bit further. There are two things that artists dare to do, it seems to me, that you can only sustain if you ultimately believe that life is a gift, not an achievement. First, they play. We use that word specifically of musical artists. But it is really true of all art. It is play. It can be very serious play, it can be play that takes years of practice to master—but it is play all the same. It is not fully adult to play. I watch my children at play and I can't help thinking of how little they know about the brokenness and danger of the world, how innocent they are of what will be required of them as they come of age and work, suffer, grieve, and die. How can you play in a world like this world? It is almost an offense—unless, in spite of the grave condition of our world, our world is still a place of grace.

And yet the other terribly useless thing that artists do is to enter into pain, and to bring us into contact with pain. In Western art this begins, as it should, with meditations on the crucified Christ. I was in Boston's Museum of Fine Arts a few weeks before the gathering in Austin, and I couldn't help noticing that people's pace quickened when they came to the rooms housing the medieval, and especially Spanish, art that dwells in dark tones on the dereliction of Christ. They were

40

moving rapidly along to the Impressionist room, where they were happy to linger among Claude Monet's bright pastel lilies and cathedrals. But Monet's work is less glibly beautiful when you know his story. He loved Camille Doncieux—the subject of his first widely recognized painting, *The Woman in the Green Dress*. They had a child in 1867, they married in 1870, had a second child in 1878, and in 1879 she died of tuberculosis at age thirty-two. In response, Monet created one of his most haunting paintings, *Camille on Her Deathbed*, in which the young woman, already drawn and pale, seems to be vanishing before our eyes into a whirlwind of nonbeing. Even our beloved Impressionist Monet painted from a place of pain.

Play and pain are two perfectly useless things, and strangely enough, they have to go together. Play can become escapism when we determinedly play on to avoid facing pain. There is a kind of art that is too easy, too willing to let us off the hook, too comforting and too culpably ignorant of what exactly grace costs. At the moment, we find this most often in the bestselling art of the Christian subculture than in the secular art worlds, but it has had its day in even the most secular venues. Pain, meanwhile, can become sadism and masochism when it is unmoored from any hope of grace, so that the artist begins to conceive his job as an endless cynical flagellation of himself and his audience. Difficulty becomes the only test of seriousness, and "decorative" becomes the only remaining swear word.

We who are privileged enough to live in North America live in a world that is forgetting both pain and play. Our popular culture offers us endless diverting amusements that fall flat and well short of real celebration. Our so-called serious culture offers us endlessly difficult dead ends. Who will be the people who can play gracefully, unusefully, in the world? Who will be the people who turn unafraid toward pain? Who will be the people who believe in beauty without being afraid of brokenness? Who will be the people who champion that which is not useful?

Ours is the age of the economist and the evolutionary biologist, each of whom have gotten very busy explaining why everything we thought was particularly human is actually just useful. Religion just turns out to be economically and evolutionarily useful. Charity and generosity—useful. Sex—useful, merely useful. And in the realm of literary and artistic criticism, it turns out that art and literature too were just expressions of power and domination—useful. Music—useful. Once you have lost the idea that the world is a gift, that culture is a gift, that culture can be taken, blessed, broken, and given, all any of it is, is useful. And then, eventually, this is all you can make of human beings—useful.

At stake in our attitude toward art, toward the beautiful, broken, unuseful parts of culture, is ultimately our attitude about those creatures that the Lord God formed out of the dust. Without a reason to believe in the unuseful, who will be left to champion those people who are not useful? People who cannot be substituted for one another, who are stubbornly and particularly themselves, in bodies capable of immense beauty and immense brokenness, capable of the most graceful play and the most terrible pain. Who will value them in those bodies? If not the church, then who?

Play and pain—feasting and fasting—these are the calling, not just of the Christian artist, but of the Christian. We bend our lives toward the recognition of Christ's body, beautiful and broken, at play and in pain. The real challenge for the church in its relationship to the arts is not to make some technical adjustments in how we do our art or how we pastor artists. The challenge is to discover Christ taking, blessing, breaking, giving. To become just slightly more the kind of people who could be like Christ and take, bless, break, and give where we are. To rekindle our capacity to be beautifully unuseful to God.

For Further Reading

Albert Borgmann, *Technology and the Character of Contemporary Life: A Philosophical Inquiry* (Chicago: University of Chicago Press, 1987)

Andy Crouch, *Culture Making: Recovering Our Creative Calling* (Downers Grove, IL: InterVarsity, 2008)

Makoto Fujimura, River Grace, www.rivergrace.com. See also Makoto Fujimura, "River Grace," *Image: A Journal of the Arts and Religion* 22 (1999)

Richard J. Mouw, *When the Kings Come Marching In: Isaiah and the New Jerusalem* (Grand Rapids: Eerdmans, 2002)

Dorothy Sayers, *The Mind of the Maker* (San Francisco: Harper & Row, 1987)

Ebbenson Davis, "Chorus." Turned hollow forms, hardwood.

The Worship

How Can Art Serve the Corporate Worship of the Church?

JOHN D. WITVLIET

For the past nine years, it has been my privilege to learn from dozens of congregations in several Christian traditions supported by the Worship Renewal Grants Program at the Calvin Institute of Christian Worship. Each year, we issue an open invitation for congregations to apply for small grants for a variety of educational and renewal programs related to worship. Each year, we receive around one hundred fifty applications from a very diverse pool of congregations for an equally diverse range of proposed programs. Taken together, these applications offer an instructive window into grassroots North American Christianity, allowing us to see strategies and approaches to worship renewal that are important enough to individual congregations to lead them to prepare a proposal.[1]

Not surprisingly, many proposals focus on the arts in worship. Proposals arrive with innovative ideas for programs related to music, dance, drama, poetry, preaching, sculpture, stained glass, textiles, and more. In fact, the percentage of arts-related proposals has steadily increased over the nine years of the program, a small quantifiable confirmation of the renewed vitality of Christian engagement with the arts.[2]

Many of the proposals we receive are well grounded, innovative, and inspiring. Yet some proposals, particularly some of the arts-related proposals, are puzzling. For even though we specify that programs must be designed to deepen and strengthen public communal worship practices, a significant number of our arts-related proposals center around arts festivals, art gallery exhibitions, after-school programs, or new commissions of various kinds which are nearly quarantined from the congregation's weekly public worship assembly. These proposals are focused on the arts themselves more than on worship renewal. Despite our attempts to prompt explicit reflection on the nature of communal worship, these proposals offer little evidence of reflection on the specific kinds of artistic expression that most promise to deepen public worship, and little awareness of the long history of Christian reflection on this topic.

Now perhaps some of these problems are the result of proposals generated by professional arts-related grant writers who happened upon our website while scouring the internet for funding sources. Yet for the most part, the proposals do not bear evidence of this. Rather, the proposals give ample evidence of two persistent themes: first, a deep awareness that the arts have so much more to offer the Christian community than we have realized, and second, a lack of awareness or imagination about how the arts might function in public worship assemblies.

Let me be very clear in saying that I appreciate and heartily endorse the role of artists and the arts in every facet of

Christian life. I cheer when the other writers in the volume speak about the arts in schools, festivals, galleries, homes, cafés, workplaces, theaters, concert venues, and museums. But alongside all of this activity is another role for the arts that is worth some of our best energy: namely, to express, challenge, and deepen our corporate acts of worship.

To further specify the limits and range of my topic, consider the meaning of the term *worship*. This term is arguably asked to do a bit too much work in Christian usage. *Worship* can refer to (1) a God-pleasing and God-focused life orientation, as in references to "24-7 worship" or "worship in all of life"; (2) a public assembly of the church, a "worship" service; or (3) an explicit act of adoration or praise, inside or outside of any public worship service, whether through sung, spoken, or enacted prayer or introspective reflection. Each of these three meanings are significant and attested to in Scripture. Each meaning is important to this volume. For example, we want artworks, artists, and artistry that emerges out of a life of worship. We celebrate and affirm how a gallery-hop or a concert function as acts of worship. We also want artworks that both express and evoke explicit acts of adoration.

In this essay, I want to probe the role of the arts in public assemblies of Christians who gather for corporate acts of praise, confession, lament, thanksgiving, proclamation, baptism, and eucharist. I do so not only because it is my assigned topic but because it is both a crucial and endangered topic.

The Crucial Nature of This Topic

It is crucial because public worship assemblies have been the cradle of so much of the very best artistry for well over three thousand years. Think, for starters, about Psalm texts, Gregorian chant melodies, the architecture of Gothic and Baroque worship spaces, the carefully crafted sermons of thousands of unknown preachers, the hymn-poems of Watts and Wesley,

the music of Bach and Palestrina, as well as paintings, tapestries, and sculptures of thousands of unnamed artists. All
of this is not just any sacred or devotional art. It is *liturgical*
art, art designed for public, corporate assemblies.[3]

This topic is also crucial because art for public worship assemblies features certain excellencies that are often unnamed
and underappreciated. Hymnologist Erik Routley once defined
hymns as "songs for unmusical people to sing together . . .
[and] such poetry as unliterary people can utter together."[4]
At first, this might seem to exult in the lack of artistry. But
Routley was actually writing to appreciate the remarkable skill
of poets and musicians who accept the challenge to be both
profound and accessible at the same time, which is a lot more
difficult than simply being one or the other. While there is a
kind of beauty in a carefully-honed studio recording, there is
another kind of beauty—an often remarkable and haunting
beauty—in the sound of a congregation of mostly unmusical
people singing together. The same is true for the full appro-
priation of other artforms in public worship assemblies.

The Endangered Nature of This Topic

Yet a focus on art for public worship assemblies is also an
endangered topic. It is nearly inaudible in certain conversations that mark the recent resurgence of interest in the arts
in the life of the church. Arguably, the majority of recent
energy around the arts has focused on artworks outside of
public worship.[5] This makes it very difficult for artists, pastors,
and congregations to imagine good possibilities for arts that
contribute to public assemblies for worship, particularly in
Christian traditions with little experience with or historical
reflection upon the role of arts in worship.

So let us consider now the arts in public worship assemblies. What makes for the most fitting expressions? In what
ways can the different art media enhance our corporate

worship? Let me offer three primary principles that would describe exemplary liturgical art. These principles aim to harvest some of the most fruitful work in liturgical aesthetics throughout the history of the church in a way that leads to some generative questions to guide local congregations and artists in imagining art that is fitting for public worship.[6]

1. Corporate Artwork and the Resistance to Isolation

The first principle is that *the most fitting liturgical arts express and deepen the corporate nature of a Christian way of life and worship*. Christianity is a first-person-plural enterprise; it is more about a "we" than a "me." It is about a people, rich in diversity, who are united in love, faith, and witness. This is why Christian worship for two thousand years has been practiced as a public, communal action. In public worship, we sing, pray, listen, and receive God's gifts together. In worship, a congregation is greater than the sum of the individuals in the room.[7]

In our own era, this communal character of Christianity is under threat in the individualistic, privatistic orientation of Western culture. There are constant temptations to reduce Christianity to a private experience that avoids any sustained contact with others. In this context, artists have some of the most potent anti-individualism medicine available: the aesthetic tools necessary to shape experiences of profound solidarity and interpersonal discipleship.

Indeed, one of the most joyfully subversive questions a liturgical artist can ask is, simply: "How might my artistic contribution resist individualism and strengthen the communal dimension of worship?" There are three possible answers to this question in each facet of the artistic experience: its reception, its content, and its production.

Reception

The easiest of these facets to probe is arguably the corporate *reception* of liturgical artworks. Hymns are designed for congregations to sing together. Well-crafted prayers or Psalms are prepared for congregations to pray together. Sermons are designed for corporate listening. Thoughtful liturgical visual artworks are prepared for people to see together. To be sure, postmodern theorists remind us that even when people experience the very same artwork at the very same time, they might well be having very different private experiences of that artwork, depending on their personality type and whatever they happened to eat for breakfast that morning. Still, the best liturgical art functions to overcome our isolation, to help us realize a corporate identity.

This means that accessibility—a dangerous and controversial criterion for artists—is a significant and legitimate factor in preparing and evaluating art for worship. Pastors are taught to prepare sermons that can be meaningful to young and old, rich and poor, brand new and lifelong worshipers, and people with various ethnicities, personality types, and backgrounds. This is also a worthy goal for all musicians, dancers, artists, and dramatists who are called to serve a worshiping congregation.

This does not mean that every excellent liturgical artwork needs to be a kind of "least common denominator" expression. The best artworks, while accessible to many, also reward repeated exposure over time. And as with songs and sermons, not every artwork can speak for or to everyone.[8]

But artists also need to hear a call to harness the power, nuance, and force of their work in ways that promise to deepen corporate reception. Some of the best liturgical artwork has arisen from genius-level artists choosing to focus their talents on producing texts and artworks that ordinary people can appropriate. Ralph Vaughan Williams wrote magnificent symphonies and song cycles, but he also was a master of harmonizing folk hymn tunes for use in out-of-the-way parish churches. Karl Barth delved into the most complex and thorny philosophical and theological debates, and yet reserved some of his most refined rhetoric for very accessible sermons to prisoners. This kind of artist is a master of works that are simple, but never simplistic; childlike, but never childish.[9] I commend to us, then, that the ability to promote corporate reception is a wise and trustworthy goal for all artists to pursue.

Content

Second, a significant amount of exemplary liturgical art takes the corporate character of a Christian way of life as its main content. So, for example, the architecture of the Calvin College Chapel, like thousands of other recently constructed spaces, calls attention to the gathering of the community around the Word, font, and table.

The architecture of Antioch Baptist Church in Perry County, Alabama, calls attention to the unity of the living and the dead as part of the one church of Jesus Christ.

Nancy Chinn's "A Year with Africa" banner installation for a congregation in Ames, Iowa, creates a powerful visual reminder that Christians in North America worship in unity with Christians in Africa.

A congregation in Hamilton, Ontario, demonstrated unity of the generations through a mixed-media community art project that incorporated objects representing the various generations in the congregation. When finished, the series of projects spelled out "One Body."

Laura James's "Psalm 100" depicts the corporate character of Christian assemblies for worship, resisting any individualistic notion of praise.

Brian Wren's evocative hymn for the Lord's Supper begins in the first person singular, but ends in the first person plural—a poetic journey that unveils the significance of the Lord's Table for uniting us in Christ with a host of people unlike ourselves in every other way.

> I come with joy to meet my Lord,
> forgiven, loved, and free;
> in awe and wonder to recall
> his life laid down for me.
>
> I come with Christians far and near
> to find, as all are fed,
> the new community of love
> in Christ's communion bread.
>
> As Christ breaks bread and bids us share,
> each proud division ends;
> the love that made us, makes us one,
> and strangers now are friends.

And thus with joy we meet our Lord;
his presence, always near,
is in such friendship better known:
we see and praise him here.

Together met, together bound,
we'll go our different ways;
and as his people in the world,
we'll live and speak his praise.[10]

Each of these works, and hundreds of others, focus on rescuing us from the individualistic orientation of our culture and both conveying and enacting the corporate content of Christian worship.

Production

Third, the corporate character of Christianity can also inform the way art is produced for worship. Many of our models of artistic creativity and production are individualistic. When we think of liturgical artists, we often picture an isolated painter in a studio, an isolated preacher in a study, an isolated musician in a practice room, an isolated songwriter in a coffeehouse.

Yet there are many more communal possibilities for artistic engagement. I know of one effective preacher who leads a group Bible study on a sermon text for the following Sunday and regularly includes insights from the group in the Sunday sermon—making the sermon the direct result of a communal act of preparation.[11] Artist Nancy Chinn very intentionally engages congregation members in the process of conceiving of and constructing fabric installations.[12] Songs and liturgical resources from the Iona community are produced by a group of musicians and textwriters, the Wild Goose Group, who work together in an intentional process of group creativity and accountability.[13] In other parts of the world, the idea of an individual songwriter or artist establishing his or her own identity independent from the community is nearly

54

inconceivable. Songs and images are literally born out of the entire congregation.

In summary, in the face of rampant individualism, the liturgical arts offer remarkable possibilities for realizing the fundamentally communal nature of the church and a Christian way of life. The best liturgical art expands our awareness and experience of the church as a functioning corporate body that transcends time and place.

2. Covenantal Artwork and the Resistance to Sentimentality

A second principle is: *the most fruitful liturgical artworks are never ends in themselves but rather function as means to deepen the covenantal relationship between God and the gathered congregation.*

Consider two lists of verbs that describe what happens in worship:

List A: seeing, listening, touching, gesturing, smelling, imagining, speaking, singing

List B: praising, lamenting, confessing, thanking, being convicted, being inspired, being comforted

List A are verbs that focus on embodied sensory experience, the rudiments of artistic production and reception. These words are not unique to worship. They are building blocks for all human actions. We can not worship without these verbs. And they are the reason that the arts matter in worship: the arts elevate, deepen, and sharpen each of these basic sensory actions and prime them as acts of worship.

List B catalogues actions that constitute the covenantal relationship Christians have with God in Jesus Christ through the Spirit. They are metaphorical terms drawn from the realm of interpersonal human relationships, which Scripture uses

55

to depict the way we know and experience God. The list includes both active verbs (praising, lamenting, confessing, thanking) and passive verbs (being convicted, inspired, and comforted) to highlight how our relationship with God is dialogic, comprising both messages we communicate to God in prayer, and messages God communicates to us through Scripture and the nourishment offered at the Lord's table. These covenantal actions are modeled for us in the Psalms, protected fiercely by the prophets, and exemplified in the most faithful examples of Christian worship over the past twenty-plus centuries.[14]

Art of the covenant

These two lists, each indispensable for worship, are related in a very simple way: the list A verbs help us accomplish list B actions. For example, in corporate worship we view an artwork in order to praise or confess. We sing in order to thank or to lament. The list A verbs help us realize the ultimate purpose of worship. As embodied human actions, these list A verbs have enormous potential to make our interaction with the Triune God more real and evocative. As Nicholas Wolterstorff has persuasively argued, "Good liturgical art is art that serves effectively the actions of the liturgy. . . . Liturgical art, much of it participatory in character, is the art of a community, at the service of its liturgical actions and not at the service of aesthetic contemplation."[15] This is a remarkably deep goal, or *telos*, for artistic engagement. The goal of the liturgical artist is not to generate artworks that merely "connect with" people, but rather to enable them, corporately, to participate in acts of trinitarian covenantal renewal.

Many of worship's largest problems occur when the connection between these list A and list B actions is unclear. When worshipers finish a song and simply think, "What a powerful, driving rhythm," or when worshipers see a colorful banner and think, "What vivid colors," then artworks have not lived up to their highest potential in their corporate context. Instead, liturgical artists should want to hear worshipers say, "Truly your song, your poetry, your dance helped us to pray, to hear God, to know and love God."

In this way, liturgical artworks promise to deepen a congregation's participation in the profoundly relational and covenantal acts of public worship, provided that artists and congregations actively resist the temptation to make artworks ends in themselves. The shift into this deeper mode of engagement requires intentionality and often a willingness to set aside some of the conventions of artistic engagement that arise in the contemporary art world. Consider several examples.

Here liturgical dancers participate in worship not by simply "performing a number" but intentionally calling attention to the grace-filled message of baptism by carrying a baptismal bowl just after words of assurance are read from Scripture.

Here a drama troupe participates not merely by rendering a skit in the middle of a service, but by enacting the Scripture reading for the day.

Here a work of pottery is created out of shards of clay that members of the congregation bring forward as a part of their own prayers of penitence and confession—shards which, when assembled, will become the table that welcomes worshipers later in the service to the Lord's Supper.

Here a piece of music is not merely "presented in worship," but is rather embedded inside a prayer. The congregation is asked not merely to listen to the music but to pray through it.

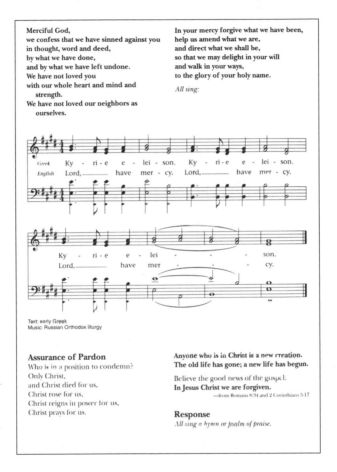

In each of these examples, an artist is pausing to ask some very basic questions: What covenantal action(s) does this artwork help this congregation engage in? Is this artwork well suited to the task? A significant number of worship-related artworks that fail in a significant way can be traced back to an artist that fails to ask these very basic questions—and to communities that never invite or expect artists to do so. These problems are not limited to artists, of course. The very same problem afflicts preachers whose speaking ultimately serves to accomplish something other than the proclamation of the gospel.

Fortunately, this kind of covenantal engagement can be cultivated in very simple, accessible ways. Many artistic commissions in the church would be much, much more serviceable if they would be formulated as adaptations of this sentence: "Please compose a piece of music or drama or dance or visual artwork in order to help this congregation in this time and place engage in X kind of covenantal activity." For example: "Please compose a song to help us at Community Church learn how to more deeply lament the hunger in our community." "Please prepare a dance that will help the pastors at First Church proclaim the remarkable message of the Prodigal Son narrative."

Resisting sentimentality

This covenantal criterion is also crucial for interrogating one of the greatest "sins" of liturgical artwork: that of sentimentality. Sentimental art invites worshipers into a mode of engagement that ultimately cheapens, rather than deepens, the enactment of their covenantal relationship with God. Sentimental artworks, as Jeremy Begbie explains, avoid depicting evil honestly, generate a kind of emotional self-indulgence, and fan an aversion to costly action and engagement.[16] As many artists will quickly attest, Christian worship seems to be a perennial magnet for attracting sentimental artworks—melodies, images, metaphors, rhythms, and palettes of color that succeed at making worship pleasant and utterly innocuous.[17]

The pastoral challenge that nearly all artistically-oriented congregations face is that of finding a constructive way to call forth works of art that avoid sentimentality. One of the best strategies is making sure that the liturgical (covenantal)

purpose of a given artwork is clear from the start. Congregations who ask a videographer or a poet to produce a work
to help the congregation "pray honestly for the needs of the
world in our intercessory prayer" are far less likely to wind
up with sentimentalist (self-referential) art than one who
merely says, "Give us something to warm up the early part
of the service" or "Let's see if we can find a home for the
artwork you have already created."

In sum, what the church needs are examples of liturgical art
that are clearly tied to specific acts of covenantal engagement:
praise, lament, confession, listening for comfort, listening for
correction. And we need artworks that resist any devolution
of those actions into sentimentalist behavior, where the sentiment of the worshiper replaces the more primary encounter
with God from which all else flows.

3. Iconic Artwork and the Resistance to Idolatry

The third and final principle is this: *the best liturgical artworks are iconic and idolatry-resisting*. When the Psalms
testify about liturgical experience, they often speak about the
worshiper contemplating nothing less than the beauty and
glory of God: "So I have looked upon you in the sanctuary,
beholding your power and glory" (Ps. 63:2), and "We ponder
your steadfast love, O God, in the midst of your temple" (Ps.
48:9). One possible exception to this pattern, the rapturous
words about the beauty of the courts of the Lord in Psalm
84:1, "How lovely is your dwelling place," uses the temple
here as a figure of speech. The second half of verse 2 points
to the Psalmist's ultimate desire for nothing less than God:
"My heart and my flesh cry out for the living God" (NIV).
Though worship is clearly an embodied, multisensory experience, what is significant in worship is that all of this sensory
experience contributes to a perception of the beauty, love,
and grace of the Triune God.

61

Iconography

One tradition that clarifies the range of perception is the Orthodox tradition of iconography. As Orthodox Christians regularly explain, their icons are not meant to be merely looked *at*. They are to be looked *through*. We affix our eyes on the image, but our hearts and minds perceive something richer and deeper through them. We perceive something of God's own beauty, love, and grace. This is what it means for art to function in an iconic way.

"Iconic" is a fitting criterion for all liturgical art. As art, it engages our senses and bodies and, while it remains an irreducibly sensory experience, it simultaneously invites us to perceive the beauty of God. Iconic engagement, in this broad sense, has long been a staple of theological reflection on the liturgical arts. In his commentary on Old Testament worship practices, John Calvin argued:

> It was not enough for the faithful, in those days, to depend upon the Word of God, and to engage in those ceremonial services which he required, unless, aided by *external* symbols, they *elevated* their *minds* above these, and yielded to God *spiritual* worship. God, indeed, gave real tokens of his presence in that visible sanctuary, but not for the purpose of binding the senses and thoughts of his people to earthly elements; he wished rather that these *external* symbols should serve as *ladders*, by which the faithful might *ascend* even to heaven.[18]

John Wesley's famous directions for congregational singing conclude with this stirring summons:

> Above all sing spiritually. Have an eye to God in every word you sing. Aim at pleasing him more than yourself, or any other creature. In order to do this attend strictly to the sense of what you sing, and see that your heart is not carried away with the sound, but offered to God continually; so shall your singing be such as the Lord will approve here, and reward you when he cometh in the clouds of heaven.[19]

In both Calvin and Wesley, and in dozens of other significant works in the history of the church, the aim is the same: to attend to, to contemplate, to savor, to adore the sheer goodness of God, of Father, Son, and Holy Spirit. In this tradition, the greatest compliment that a worshiper can offer an artist is not, "What a remarkably engaging artwork you offered us" (which is fine on its own), but rather, "Through your work, we gained a new glimpse of God's character, the person of Jesus, the work of the Holy Spirit."

Resisting idolatry

But if the liturgical arts invite us to contemplate God, then they are charged with one of the most serious tasks in the entire Christian community: resisting idolatrous concepts and images of God. Indeed, the arts are not only a potent antidote to individualism and sentimentality, they are also a potent and constructive agent for resisting idolatries.

This is not the usual linkage of the "arts" and "idolatry." Usually, when these terms appear together, it is in the context of anxiety about how the arts will lead to idolatry—especially the idolatry of the artwork or artist. This traditional concern has fueled iconoclastic movements throughout the history of the church, sometimes drawing on the second commandment's prohibition of graven images for God.

But the idolizing of artists and artworks is not the only form of idolatry that haunts the Christian life. There is another, sometimes more insidious form of idolatry—an idolatry of distortion. We worship an idol not only when we treat an object as if it were God, but also when we conceive of divine life, divine glory, and divine redemption in sub-Christian ways, in ways that do not live up to the rich biblical depictions of God's being and character. My songwriter colleague Greg Scheer has invited congregations to sing, "Show us some new facet of yourself, some truth, that breaks the idols we have made of you."[20] The arts are one way that God's Spirit can and does answer that prayer.

Consider several liturgical artworks that aim at resisting idolatry. First, consider this hymn and anthem text by the Iona Community's John Bell.

> Lift up your heads, eternal gates, Alleluia!
> See how the King of glory waits, Alleluia!
> The Lord of Hosts in drawing near,
> the Savior of the world is here, Alleluia!
>
> But not in arms or battle dress, Alleluia!
> God comes, a child, amidst distress, Alleluia!
> No mighty armies shield the way,
> only coarse linen, wool, and hay, Alleluia!
>
> God brings a new face to the brave, Alleluia!
> God redefines who best can save, Alleluia!
> Not those whose power relies on threat,
> terror or torture, destruction or debt, Alleluia!
>
> God's matchless and majestic strength, Alleluia!
> In all its height, depth, breadth, and length, Alleluia!
> Now is revealed, its power to prove,
> by Christ protesting, "God is love," Alleluia![21]

This is a text of resistance. It attempts to correct the myopic perception that salvation comes best through human power structures. At the same time, the text subverts any notion of God that is degraded by a too raw-fisted concept of divine power.

Second, consider the painting on the facing page by four-year-old artist Maura Cronin, entitled "Jesus Happy and Sad." This painting clearly resists various sentimental images and icons that depict Jesus as merely a kindly friend or an overly sanguine companion.

Third, consider this remarkable liturgical space, the Chapel on the Water in Hokkaido, Japan. This space invites introspective reflection and bears the influence of mystical Eastern traditions. However, the mysticism promoted here is

not ahistorical mysticism in which the worshiper attempts to set aside all reflection on specific, concrete historical actions in order to contemplate an eternal nothingness. Rather, this space calls the worshiper to deep, introspective contemplation of the very historical event of the cross.

The church's long resistance to the arts in worship arises in part because of its deep (and valid) concern about idolatry. The arts, like any area of human achievement, can quickly become idolatrous. But the arts can also be an effective tool of resistance—a potent antidote to imagining God in idolatrous ways.

Now any artist who sets out to displace idolatrous conceptions of God—like any theologian, preacher, or pastoral

65

caregiver who attempts the same—will quickly discover the spiritual dangers that accompany the prophetic task. Being asked to help a congregation perceive God's glory more truly can easily lead to a self-righteous attitude about the truth that we artists, or we theologians, or we preachers, think we possess. This means that every aspiring liturgical artist, like every pastor, preacher, and theologian, needs to practice the kinds of spiritual disciplines that will resist this kind of self-righteousness, and participate in relationships of spiritual accountability and discernment. Ultimately, resisting idolatry, like worship itself, is a task for a community to engage in.

But when this kind of spiritual discernment and account-ability is in place, artists rightly assume a potent prophetic and priestly task of helping a congregation perceive the glory of the Triune God. This stunning claim means that "resisting idolatry" is one of the essential callings for every aspiring liturgical artist. Such an artist is invited to name which idol of the imagination we are eager to resist and which aspects of divine beauty we are eager to highlight (and adore!).

Conclusion

In summary, then, the most fitting liturgical artwork is one that is corporate, covenantal, and iconic. Each of these criteria invites artists to new modes of creativity and engagement with the community of which they are a part. Each of them warrants a kind of disciplined attention by pastors, church leaders, artists, and the larger congregation. This can be ac-complished by probing some very basic questions:

- How can the making of a liturgical artwork be accom-plished in a communal way?
- How might my artistic gifts testify to the corporate character of the Christian faith?

- How can my artwork speak to the wide range of people in the congregation, and what can I do to enable worshipers to understand and experience this artwork more deeply?
- What can I do so that my artwork is not merely admired (or dismissed!), but rather is experienced as an act of prayer or proclamation?
- What can I do so that my people see through (or "listen through") my artwork to perceive the beauty and glory of God?
- What distorted notion of God's beauty and character can my artwork resist? What neglected positive quality of God's beauty can my artwork highlight?

None of these questions need squelch creativity. But they can serve to discipline creativity—a discipline that emerges out of a rich, theological understanding of worship and the Christian life. May God's Spirit strengthen, inspire, and challenge artists of all kinds to take up their prophetic and priestly tasks among God's worshiping people.

For Further Reading

Frank Burch Brown, *Inclusive, Yet Discerning: Navigating Worship Artfully* (Grand Rapids: Eerdmans, 2009)

William A. Dyrness, *Senses of the Soul: Art and the Visual in Christian Worship* (Eugene, OR: Cascade Books, 2008)

Christopher Irvine, *The Art of God: The Making of Christians and the Meaning of Worship* (Chicago: Liturgy Training Publications, 2005)

Catherine Kapikian, *Art in Service of the Sacred* (Nashville: Abingdon, 2006)

Don E. Saliers, *Worship Come to Its Senses* (Nashville: Abingdon, 1996)

Baker Galloway, "Just Trying to Get By." Varnished tempera on watercolor board.

The Art Patron

*Someone Who Can't Draw a Straight Line
Tries to Defend Her Art-Buying Habit*

LAUREN F. WINNER

Five years ago, I was asked a question about art I have not been able to shake. The setting: a lecture hall at a small Christian school in the northeast. I had been asked to give a lecture about memoir. The talk went pretty well, and many people in the audience had read *Girl Meets God*, the memoir that recounts a year shortly after my conversion from Judaism to Christianity. Afterward, one of the audience members approached me. She said that she had enjoyed my book and had learned a lot about Judaism from it. But she was very disturbed by one passage, which she flipped to in her copy of the book. It was marked by a big black "X" in the margin, and an even bigger black question mark.

The passage in question was my discussion of the first time I ever spent money on art, which was a papercutting of Ruth 1:21 by a contemporary Jewish artist named Diane Palley.[1] I purchased this papercutting at a very particular moment: a season in which I was trying to understand what kind of relationship (if any) I could still have with Judaism; a time during which, in ways not always easy to articulate, I deeply mourned my own rejection of the Judaism in which I had grown up. In the midst of that mourning, the Book of Ruth came to have a lot of meaning for me. Ruth is, after all, a story about conversion. I found myself pondering Ruth's place with her new family and people and wondering about the losses she had sustained on her way there. I paid nine hundred dollars for Diane Paley's papercutting. It still hangs by my bed as part of an effort to make sense of my conversion and the losses it entailed.

That was the passage from *Girl Meets God* my interlocutor found troubling—my description of buying the papercutting. She said she was disturbed by my willingness to spend that much money on a piece of art. I think that she felt I was too glib and flippant in narrating that purchase, that I hadn't demonstrated any awareness of the privilege entailed in dropping the equivalent of two months' rent on a piece of art. "How, in terms of Christian ethics," she asked, "can you justify spending that money on art when there are poor people to be fed?"

I have pondered her question many, many times. Nine hundred dollars is a lot of money to a broke grad student. Nine hundred dollars is a lot of money for just about anyone (except perhaps for the artist who had to buy the paper, pay for health insurance, and generally keep body and soul together). The woman's concern that one perhaps ought not to spend extravagantly on art when there are poor people to be fed is, it seems to me, both insightful and problematic. It is a variation of a long-standing trope that tacitly criticizes the excesses of European cathedrals. Money for stained-glass windows? Gold altars? Elaborate stone carvings? When there are starving children around the corner? Scandalous! This is just one of the themes that has given many in the world—and many in the church—the impression that Christians, or at least Protestants, are hostile to "the arts."

At the same time, there was, in my interlocutor's concern, an important challenge. To be honest—and this is not language I use very often—I think the Holy Spirit was speaking to me through that woman. I do *not* think the Holy Spirit was telling me never to spend money on art. But the conversation was an absolute awakening to my own privilege. Art requires a person to pay the artist, and on occasion I have been *privileged* to be that person. I honestly often do not know what to do about that privilege.

I tried for a two-pronged response: on one hand, to take my interlocutor seriously as a messenger speaking on behalf of the God who became poor himself, and on the other, to undertake my obligations to that God and to the poor people in my neighborhood within the framework of what we might call a Eucharistic ethics of abundance. The God who impoverished himself is also the God of abundance, and somehow, perhaps at times nonsensically, Christians are called to live out of an ethic not of scarcity, but of abundance—an abundance that extends both to the homeless neighbor and to the artist neighbor. Beyond that, there is always a bit of self-justification involved when I purchase art. I can hardly call myself a "patron," but there is a certain satisfaction in knowing that my one splurge purchase of the year has gone to support an artist who, in all likelihood, is struggling to make ends meet and to make art.

And then there is this. The next time I feel like purchasing art, perhaps I should make that purchase with and for my community by buying a piece of art with and for my local church, for example. Or at the very least, I should take the art that hangs in my house as one more prompt to hospitality. I love the paintings on my walls, and I should share them with other people by welcoming people into my home.

I feel uncomfortable even writing about this. It's embarrassing to talk about money, embarrassing to talk about having the money to buy a painting or a papercutting. It's one thing to talk in an abstract or even theological way about "supporting the arts." It's quite another to talk about actually having written a check for a piece of sculpture or a tapestry or a nineteenth-century silhouette. This is a very concrete, practical piece of what it means for the church to support the arts: people with disposable income choosing to spend money on art; people budgeting and saving and supporting artists; people, like me, deciding not to buy clothes for a year so that they can purchase a painting. (And you see what I just did, don't you? I have tried to apologize for and soften this topic by assuring you that I don't just throw money around thoughtlessly on art—I scrape and save for it!)

This essay is not just an apologia for buying papercuttings, though it is also that. It is a brief exploration of why it is I care about art and a reminder of how and why the church may—and in fact *does*—care about art too.

67 Stratford Road

I grew up in two contexts that decisively shaped my understanding of art. The first context was my family and my childhood home. Both of my parents, without pretense, were interested in visual arts. Neither claimed much expertise, but art was one of the few extravagances in our household. There were paintings on the walls and thick, glossy-paged art books on the bookshelves and coffee tables. To this day, my father searches on eBay for various artistic objects he likes. (One year it was kachina dolls; this year it is Louis Orr's etchings of historic North Carolina buildings.) As a child, beyond protesting when my parents dragged me to a museum, I didn't think much about all this art. On the contrary, I simply took for granted the presence of art in homes.

To my mind, becoming an adult was synonymous not with drinking alcohol or buying a car, but with acquiring art. When I turned eighteen, my mother, who usually gave me a sweater or a coat for my October birthday, told me she wanted to give me something special. She had in mind a nice set of earrings. But I wanted something different. I wanted a painting called "The Meeting" which had been painted in 1986 by an artist named Saralyn Spradling from my hometown. The eponymous "meeting" was a Junior League meeting, and smack in the middle of the seven-foot-long canvas was an image of my mother, one-time president of the Asheville Junior League. I don't think I had ever actually seen the painting. But I remembered a grainy black-and-white photograph of it that had run in the local newspaper some years before. (More cringing, of course, is involved in telling this story. The interlocutor who worried about how much I spent on Diane Palley's papercutting is sitting on my shoulder, raising an eyebrow: "Ahem. Fancy earrings? *The Junior League?*")

Well, my mother was taken aback. Quite simply, she thought it was extremely peculiar that she was offering jewelry and her still-teenage daughter—a daughter who most of the time wanted nothing to do with her mother—was asking instead for a giant painting that featured Mom and Mom's friends clad in pink and green and grosgrain ribbon and other 1980s garb. She tried to argue me out of my wish. Where would I put the painting? Did I really want to be saddled with it for the rest of my life? What if my taste changed? Given that I'd never actually seen this painting, was I sure I didn't want diamond studs? Finally, Mom gave up and said that if I did all the legwork—call Mrs. Spradling, see if she knew who owned the painting, find out if the owners would sell it for less than an arm and a leg—I could have "The Meeting" instead of earrings for my birthday present.

The painting hangs in my hallway today. I am not a Junior Leaguer myself, but I remember my mother's work in the League vividly and I find something quite appropriate about having this painting in my hallway—more appropriate, actually, than I knew when I originally requested the present. My mother hadn't yet told me that she went into labor with me at a Junior League meeting. Now, a decade and a half since I received "The Meeting," my mother is dead, and I am doubly glad to have this painting of her. It is, among other things, a visual genealogy, a reminder of a heritage about which I remain ambivalent.

I find that this painting makes it possible for me to contemplate something about my mother I otherwise avoid. In fact, it has been only by staring at that painting—staring intensely, absorbed, not unlike the way one might reflectively gaze upon an icon or other devotional image—that I have been able to cry since her death. Not at her funeral. Not on her death's anniversary. Only after staring for long minutes at that painting and thereby entering more fully into the story it has to tell. A story I still don't fully understand.

In the Pages of *Masechet Shabbat*

Which brings me to the second place that shaped my thinking about art: the pages of the Talmud.

In many ways, although I have been a Christian for all of my adult life, the spiritual formation that remains most basic to how I meet the world and how I try to meet God is the formation I received in the Jewish communities in which I grew up. The Jewish communities of my childhood taught me, among other things, about art. Specifically, Judaism taught me the principle of *hiddur mitzvah*. This is the idea that one does not just *do* the commandments, one "beautifies" them. The roots of this commandment may be found in Exodus 15:2, which may be translated something like: "This is my

God and I will beautify him with praises." In a passage of the Talmud (*Masechet Shabbat* 133b), the rabbis muse over this verse: What exactly does it mean to "beautify" God? How does one "beautify God with praises"? The rabbis have an answer: "Adorn yourself before him by a truly elegant fulfillment of the religious duties, for example a beautiful tabernacle, a beautiful palm branch, a beautiful ram's horn, beautiful show fringes, a beautiful scroll or the Torah, written in fine ink, with a fine reed, by a skilled penman, wrapped with beautiful silks."

In other words, when you fulfill the commandment to blow a *shofar*, a ram's horn, during the liturgies for Rosh Hashanah and Yom Kippur, don't blow just any old ram's horn—beautify the commandment by using a beautiful *shofar*. And when you build and take your meals in a *sukkah*, a hut, during the festival of Sukkot, do not just throw up a shack whose dimensions happen to meet the requirements, but build a beautiful tabernacle in which to take your holiday meals. And when you obey the commandment to put ritual fringes on your four-cornered garments, do not drape yourself in a shoddy cloth that is falling apart, but wrap yourself in a beautiful prayer shawl so that you might do honor to the God who has commanded you. This is the theological sensibility that prompted those seventeenth- and eighteenth-century eastern European Jews to craft intricate marriage contracts, turning simple legal documents into objects of art. Those papercutters knew that a man pledging to treat his soon-to-be wife fairly and honorably was more than just the faithful discharging of a commandment. It was an opportunity to "adorn"—to glorify—God.

Hiddur mitzvah has both public and domestic manifestations. It is expressed in the synagogue and in the home. When you attend Friday night dinner at the home of your Jewish neighbor, you are seeing *hiddur mitzvah* in the elegant Shabbat accoutrements: the silk challah covers, the elaborate goblets over which the blessing of wine is said, the decorative candlesticks that hold the lights one is commanded to kindle at the onset of the Sabbath. You are seeing *hiddur mitzvah* on the front door of your host's house. Jews have beautified the commandment to "Write [the commandments] on the doorframes of your houses and on your gates" (Deut. 6:9) by placing small pieces of parchment, inscribed with words of Torah, in artistic and lovely decorative cases known as *mezuzot* and nailing these *mezuzot* to their doorways for everyone to see. *Hiddur mitzvah* is also on display in synagogues—for example, in the ornate silver breastplates and crowns that decorate the Torah scrolls and in the decorative *yad*, the pointer that people use to guide them in the reading from the Torah scroll. All of this art has a purpose: its purpose is to adorn and honor God.

Perhaps a defense of my expensive book of Ruth papercutting begins with the recognition that the delicate papercutting Diane Palley sold me adorns not just my bedroom wall—it adorns God.

North American Christians and the "Beauty of Holiness"

When I became a Christian, I was struck by the vitality and intensity—and anxiety—of conversations about "Christianity and the Arts." I was struck by the number of new Christian artist friends who insisted that "Christianity" was indifferent or hostile to "the arts." Granted, there is a strain in Christian theology that is hostile to visual art—that says art is a waste of time, or an indulgence, tantamount to idolatry.[2] And Christians trying to do creative production face real challenges.

In particular, there is the challenge of community. How does artistic production from within an often tight-knit religious community work? This is a question my students and I ponder in the creative writing workshops I teach. Sometimes creative production requires violating communal norms, or at least holding your community's assumptions up to scrutiny. Sometimes it involves telling community secrets, stories the community may not want outsiders to hear, stories the community may not want to hear out loud itself. In her essay "Bringing Home the Work," poet Julia Kasdorf speaks about the difficulties of writing about the religious community of her childhood. That "community can be equivalent to friend, relative, lover, and enemy all rolled into one," she writes. "[A] transgression in language might jeopardize my status in the community."[3] Kasdorf is writing about her childhood Mennonite community, but the sentiment is one that many of us who are trying to do creative work in religious communities recognize.

At the same time—and I speak as one who did not grow up in a Christian environment that made me feel that creativity was unwelcome—from where I sit, it looks like at least some Christians in North America are remarkably supportive of the arts. Admittedly there is not the same kind of formal (and financial) ecclesial patronage for the arts that obtained in some medieval Christian communities. Yet especially in the last decade or two, there has been a real flowering of North American interest in and institutional support for art. Ironically, the number of symposia, journal articles, and informal conversations devoted to the "problem" of faith and the arts demonstrates just how much energy there is around the arts in Christian communities.

That energy around art is part of our birthright. As many in these conversations have noted, Scripture makes clear that God is interested in art. If you doubt that, turn to Exodus 26 and see how much space is devoted to the details of the tabernacle—loops of blue fabric, gold and bronze clasps, ram skin dyed red. Scripture is not the only foundation for contemporary Christian engagements with art. Such engagement is shot through the history of North American Christianity. This, actually, is something that I think a lot of contemporary, anxious conversations about "the church and the arts" get wrong. These conversations seem to presuppose that "the Christian subculture" is hostile toward something called "art." While there is such a subculture, and while one can find in it evidence of such hostility, there is also plenty of evidence that from the earliest days, North American Christians cared a lot about art.

As a wealth of fairly recent research into the visual and material culture of North American Protestantism makes clear, the caricatured plain white New England meetinghouse is not the end (or even the beginning) of the story. A different beginning may be found in the Anglican houses of worship of the early South. As Louis Nelson has recently argued, Anglicans in colonial South Carolina had a theology of beauty. They "understood earthly beauty to be a shadow of its divine original" and they preached sermons that "declared the beauty of holiness." In turn they built church buildings that expressed contemporary aesthetic virtues of "regularity, beauty, and stability." They filled those churches with finely crafted silver liturgical implements and paintings of angels that turned worshipers' imaginations to the supernatural. They worshiped in those spaces with music that, over the course of the colonial era, evolved from simple lining out of Psalms to more elaborate church music, all of which aimed both to glorify God and reflect God's glory.[4]

Anglican houses of worship are just one example of church buildings that tell us how much North American Christians care about art. We could look at other examples: the expensive churches Connecticut Congregationalists built during the early Republic that displayed fashionable neoclassical architecture; the intense polychromatic interior of Boston's Trinity Church which reflected post–Civil War theological and aesthetic innovations. And so forth.

Ecclesial architecture is not the only register on which North American Christians engaged art. Christians created and produced all manner of art within their homes. For example, Anglican girls in the early South produced artwork for their households, sewing elaborate and often quite accomplished pieces of needlework. These pieces of embroidery often featured biblical scenes—they literally interwove aesthetic pleasure and the biblical story. As David Morgan has demonstrated, visual art has long been central to Protestant devotional lives. Sunday school visionaries understood the power of pictures to draw children into religious lessons. Even ostensibly culture-avoiding premillenialists used extensive visual imagery in their charts, graphs, and Bible illustrations. More recently, mid-twentieth-century mainline Protestants sponsored art exhibits in their church fellowship halls and held panels devoted to discussing "good"—that is, modern—art.[5] The story of North American Christianity and "the arts," then, is actually one of intense engagement, an engagement that encompasses vastly different theologies (from dispensationalist to liberal) as well as vastly different aesthetic sensibilities (from didactic, mass-produced imagery to self-consciously modernist, and no less didactic, artwork).

Early-twenty-first-century Christian defenses of art often turn on enthusiasm for art's uselessness: to defend art is to defend utterly supernumerary beauty. Planet Earth, with all its seemingly purposeless aesthetic whimsy—glow-in-the-dark fish, majestic mountains, peacocks' plumage—is adduced as evidence that our creator God is interested in extravagant, useless beauty, that God made beautiful things just for kicks. Many since Kant have argued for purposeless beauty, and certainly the argument has force, especially for Christians who grew up in communities where beauty was suspect, where anything other than kneel-and-pray-the-sinner's-prayer-right-now evangelism was considered a waste of time. Apologia for senseless beauty are compelling insofar as they dissent from our society's tendency to instrumentalize and to reductively, perniciously measure everything (and everyone) in utilitarian terms.

79

But Christian defenses of art that are grounded in notions of art's very uselessness may obscure as much as they illuminate. The genealogy of North American Christian art I have sketched above suggests that very often, there *is* a purpose to art. (And to acknowledge this is not to adopt a capitalistic mindset in which "productivity" or "usefulness" is the measure of all things.) Again, consider Exodus 26. The beauty of the utensils described there honor God and set apart the rites dedicated to him. For those South Carolina Anglicans, beauty mattered because it materialized goodness and truth. The Sunday schoolers' graphs and illustrations mattered because they clarified and interpreted good, truthful texts. Even in God's creation, beauty has a purpose; in nature, beauty helps species survive.

It is important to note that sometimes art matters in ways for which we should repent. Art's effects are not always lovely; sometimes its effects are violent and sinful. Consider, for example, medieval paintings of the crucifixion (such as the fifteenth-century "Crowning with Thorns" attributed to the Master of the Karlsruhe Passion, or Matthias Grunewald's "Mocking of Christ") which, through the iconography of Jewish hats and pointed noses, depicts Jews—not Romans, but Jews—as Christ's crucifiers. This is, decidedly, art with a purpose. The purpose was to visually stage and teach deicide charges, and it was art that had consequences. It was part and parcel of creating a world in which Christians could kill Jews in retribution for the killing of Jesus.

A Christian apologia for art does not need to be—perhaps cannot be—an apologia for senseless beauty. This, it seems to me, is part of the long answer I have tried to work out to the troubling question posed to me about that nine-hundred-dollar papercutting of Ruth. A Christian understanding of art involves a recognition that art does things. In our Christian history, art *mattered*. For good and for ill, it was a key part of the Christian experience. Art had a purpose. It taught children to love the Bible. It schooled viewers in theological stories. Sometimes it incited violence. Sometimes it directed Sunday worshipers' attention heavenward.

And perhaps art can even be revelatory. *Hiddur mitzvah*, I have said, is manifested in *mezuzot* and candlesticks. It is also manifested in the Torah scroll itself. The Torahs from which Jews chant in synagogue are written in elaborate, precise calligraphy. That calligraphy is not "merely" senselessly beautiful. The rabbis teach us that the calligraphy itself contains meaning, that if only we knew how to read them, the crowns and swirls and flourishes on the calligraphed letters have something to tell us about God.

And so the command to beautify the commandments loops back on itself, staging the abundance of meaning with which truthful symbols always overflow: the beautification of the commandment itself becomes a place where God reveals himself to us—if only we take the time to linger there.

For Further Reading

Patricia Hampl, *Blue Arabesque: A Search for the Sublime* (Boston: Harvest Books, 2007)

Robin Jensen, *The Substance of Things Seen: Art, Faith, and the Christian Community* (Grand Rapids: Eerdmans, 2004)

Julia Kasdorf, *The Body and the Book: Writing from a Mennonite Life* (University Park, PA: Penn State University Press, 2009)

David Morgan and Sally M. Promey, eds., *The Visual Culture of American Religions* (Berkeley: University of California Press, 2001)

Chaim Potok, *The Gift of Asher Lev* (New York: Ballantine Books, 1997)

Laura Jennings, "Rubble #1." Acrylic on canvas.

The Pastor

How Artists Shape Pastoral Identity

EUGENE PETERSON

After I accepted the invitation to be at the symposium in Austin, I wondered, "Why me? I'm not an artist; I'm a pastor. A pretty conventional pastor at that. I study and preach the Scriptures. I lead a congregation in worship of the Father, Son, and Holy Ghost. I listen to and pray with men and women who, whether they know it or not, are called to follow Jesus in the way of the cross."

I know I would be honored to have all of those artists in my congregation. But I didn't know what I was doing there in *their* congregation or why they would have wanted me there. But after thinking along those lines for a while, it didn't take me long to realize why I was there. I was there to be a witness. I was there to give witness to the decisive and critical influence that artists have had in my life as a pastor in a Christian church.

I grew up in a small town in Montana where I never even saw an artist. The sectarian church in which I was raised was far too serious about keeping me separate from worldly contamination to waste time on artists. But beginning when I was a twenty-two-year-old theological student in New York City, artists started entering my life in ways that profoundly shaped who I was becoming as a pastor in America, where there is very little sense of the pastoral vocation (and even that "very little" is mostly wrong). I want to tell you about three of them—three artists who became my allies in developing a distinct, biblically-rooted, and church-oriented pastoral identity.

Willi Ossa

Willi Ossa was the first. Willi provided a way to understand the term *pastor* that was new to me. The term *pastor* in our American culture does not name a vocation that carries with it a clear job description. This is probably right. Jobs have job descriptions. A job is an assignment to do work that can be quantified and evaluated. It is pretty easy to decide whether a job has been completed or not. It is pretty easy to tell whether a job is done well or badly.

But a vocation is not a job in that sense. I can be hired to do a job, paid a fair wage if I do it, dismissed if I don't. But I can't be hired to be a pastor, for my primary responsibility is not to the people I serve, but to the God I serve. And as it turns out, the people I serve would often prefer an idol who would do what they want done rather than what the God revealed in Jesus wants them to do. In our present culture, the

84

sharp distinction between a job and a vocation is considerably blurred. How do I prevent myself as a pastor from thinking of my work as a job that I get paid for, a job that is assigned to me by a denomination, a job that I am expected to do to the satisfaction of my congregation? How do I stay attentive to and listen to the call that got me started in this way of life? This is not the call to help people feel good about themselves and have a good life or a call to use my considerable gifts and fulfill myself. It is a call like Abraham's, "to set out for a place . . . not knowing where he was going" (Heb. 11:8); a call to deny myself and take up my cross and follow Jesus (Matt. 16:24); a call like Jonah's to "go at once to Nineveh . . ." (Jon. 1:1), a city he detested; a call like Paul's to "get up and enter the city and you will be told what to do" (Acts 9:6). How do I keep the immediacy and authority of God's call in my ears when an entire culture, both secular and ecclesial, is giving me a job description? How do I keep the calling, the *vocation* of pastor, from being drowned out by job descriptions gussied up in glossy challenges and visions and strategies clamoring incessantly for my attention?

I have been trying for fifty years now to be a pastor in a culture that doesn't know the difference between a vocation and a job. The people who have been of most help to me in discerning this difference and embodying it in my life as a pastor have been artists. My seminary professors had no idea what pastors are or do. Only one of them had ever been a pastor, and he was an adjunct. Most of my pastor friends and colleagues since my ordination have embraced the secularized job identity of pastor that is pervasive throughout American culture. They have been less than helpful.

Willi Ossa was the first artist I ever knew personally. I was a seminary student in New York City and had been assigned to do field work at West Park Presbyterian Church on West 86th Street. The year was 1955. One of my responsibilities was to meet with a group of about thirty young adults on Friday nights. They were all from someplace else; most of them were artists who had come primarily from the South and Midwest to the city in which they hoped they would find affirmation and opportunity as artists. Most of them were dancers and singers. Two were poets. There was one sculptor. All of them had menial jobs—some were secretaries, some waiters and waitresses, one drove a taxi, another sold shoes at Macy's. But they were all serious artists. I don't know how accomplished they were in their art, but I soon realized that whatever they had to do to pay the rent and eat, none of them were defined by their jobs—they were artists, whether anyone else saw them as artists, and regardless of whether anyone would ever pay them to be artists. Being an artist was not a job. It was a way of life; it was a vocation.

I don't remember very well what we did on those Friday evenings—they weren't markedly religious or spiritual as I recall, although sometimes they asked me to talk to them about something in the Bible or about God. Most had some church background but none seemed particularly devout. The group was not intentionally formed for artists and I have no idea how they happened to find one another in that church. But there they were. And there I was, the youngest and only nonartist. When they just wanted to relax and have fun, we would square dance. I grew up in square-dancing country in Montana, but I had never seen square dancing like this—these men and women were *dancers*, I mean *real* dancers.

Willi Ossa wasn't one of the group, but he was always there. Willi was the church janitor. He was there to pick up after us and keep the place clean. But "janitor" was not who he was. "Janitor" was his job. He himself, Willi Ossa, was a painter, a serious painter. He painted mostly on canvas with oils. Something unspoken drew us together and within a month or two we were friends.

Willi was German and had married the daughter of an officer in the occupying American army in post-war Germany. He and his wife, Mary, had come to New York a couple of years before I met them. They lived with their infant daugh-

ter in a third-floor, walk-up apartment six blocks from the
church. Willi was slight of build—a wiry, intense five foot
eight. I always sensed a seething energy in him, like a volcano
about to erupt. Mary was about the same height, but lacked
the intensity. She seemed fragile, but there was a tough, ma-
ternal attentiveness just beneath the surface. The nighttime
janitorial job suited Willi because it left the days free for
painting in natural light.

It wasn't long before they were inviting me for supper on
Fridays before the evening meeting with the singles group. And
then one Friday Willi said he would like to paint my portrait.
Why didn't I come, say about four o'clock on Fridays, and he
would paint me for an hour or so? Then we would eat supper
and walk over to the church together.

In the weeks of our getting acquainted before the portrait painting began, I had learned that Willi had a severely
negative opinion of the church. And "severely negative" is
an understatement. It was outraged hostility. He had lived
through the war and personally experienced at close quar-
ters the capitulation of the German church to Hitler and the
Nazis. His pastor had become a fervent Nazi. He had never
heard of Dietrich Bonhoeffer or Martin Neimoller or the
Karl Barth of the Barmen Confession. All he knew was that
the state of the church he had grown up in hated Jews and
embraced Hitler as a prophet. He couldn't understand why
I would be studying to be a pastor in a church. He warned
me of the evil and corrupting influence it would have on me.
He told me that churches, all churches, reduced pastors to
functionaries in a bureaucracy where labels took the place
of faces and rules trumped relationships. He liked me. He
didn't want his friend destroyed.

And then he began painting my portrait. He said that he
wanted to work in a form that was new to him. But he would
never let me see what he was painting. There was always a
cloth over the easel when I walked into his cluttered living-
room studio. Every Friday I would sit with the afternoon

sun on me, mostly silent, as he painted and Mary prepared a simple supper. Then we would walk the six blocks to the church.

One afternoon Mary came into the room, looked at the nearly finished portrait, and exclaimed, *"Krank! Krank!"* I knew just enough German to hear "Sick! Sick!" In the rapid exchange of sharp words between them, I caught Willi's *"Nicht krank, aber keine Gnade"*—"He's not sick now, but that's the way he will look when the compassion gets squeezed out of him."

A couple of weeks later the portrait was complete and he let me see it. He had painted me in a black pulpit robe, seated with a red Bible in my lap, my hands folded over it. The face was gaunt and grim, the eyes flat and without expression. I asked him about Mary's *"Krank"* comment. He said that she was upset because he had painted me as a sick man. "And what did you answer her?" "I told her that I was painting you as you would look in twenty years if you insisted on being a pastor." And then, "Eugene, the church is an evil place. No matter how good you are and how good your intentions, the church will suck the soul out of you. I'm your friend. Please, don't be a pastor."

His prophetic portrait entered my imagination and, quite truthfully, it has never faded. But I didn't follow his counsel. Eventually I did become a pastor. But I also kept that portrait in a closet in my study for fifty-five years as a warning. I still pull it out occasionally and look into those vacant eyes, Willi's prophetic portrait of the desolation he was convinced the church would visit on me if I became a pastor.

I was with those artists and Willi Ossa on Friday evenings for two years. I had never been immersed in a community of people who lived vocationally in a society in which everyone else seemed to be living a job description. They seemed to me quite unselfconscious about their vocational identity. I never heard them talk of being a "successful" artist. Their vocation didn't come from what anyone thought of them or paid them. Certainly they wanted to act and dance and sing on Broadway. And Willi would have loved to have had a showing of his paintings in one of the galleries on Madison Avenue. But their identity was vocational, a calling, not a job description.

Nothing I have heard or read in the years since has made such a deep and lasting impression on me as those two years with artists on Friday nights on West 86th Street. And it has been the artists in my life—not exclusively, but more than most others—who keep the distinction sharp between vocation and job description.

Bezalel (aka Gerry Baxter)

A few years later another artist, Bezalel, came into my life. Actually, I never met him personally. He had been dead for three thousand years when I made his acquaintance, an acquaintance that was as formative for me as a pastor as my friendship with Willi Ossa, but in a different way. Willi Ossa and the gathering of artists on Fridays on West 86th Street had clarified my sense of vocation and set me free from anything like a job-description understanding of being a pastor. Bezalel clarified another dimension of the pastoral work that I had never even noticed—the nature and urgency of worship in the life of the church and the Christian.

I was still in the early years of my formation as a pastor. I had completed my seminary training, spent a couple of years in graduate studies in Semitic languages, gotten married and begun a family, and spent another three years as an associate pastor learning the ropes of church life. And then I was called by my denomination to form a new congregation in a small community twenty miles northeast of Baltimore. I was thirty years old.

I had a lot of book learning. I had taken on responsibilities in family and church that were in the process of forming a pastoral identity in me. But I was still far from being formed. I had not yet become who I was called to be.

My wife and I spent three years gathering a core congregation in the basement of our home. We were now ready to construct a church sanctuary. While we were getting ready to do that, Bezalel came into my life. But not directly. He came mediated by Gerry Baxter. It happened like this.

The denominational office responsible for supervising the organization and development of new churches sent a consultant from a large architectural firm that specialized in churches to meet with our building committee. As the six of us sat around a table, the man began pulling church building plans out of his briefcase for us to consider: "Here's a colonial. This is historic colonial country you are living in; I think this might suit the ambience of the culture here. And here is a kind of neogothic. It has a distinctive 'church' look—it would probably attract people who don't know much about church but are looking for something solid and safe." And then another: "I think you would be interested in considering this one. It's very popular right now—a multipurpose building, easily convertible from sanctuary to church suppers to community gatherings. Very functional. Given your circumstances, I would probably recommend this."

The man left. He had been with us a little over an hour. He had not asked us a single question. He left knowing nothing about who we were or the way we understood church. We decided that all he knew of church was in those half dozen building plans in his briefcase. It took us no more than twenty minutes to agree that we weren't going to use his services. We weren't interested in selecting one of the standard options. There was more to church than a building. We needed a building. But we were not about to be reduced to a building.

What he didn't know, and didn't bother to find out, was that we had been worshiping together for three years in the house basement in which our meeting with him had just taken place. What he didn't know, and didn't bother to find out, was that we were already a church—a church in formation. We were new at this, true, but we were already well on our way in discussing the nature of worship, the nature of congregation, and the part that architecture would play in expressing and shaping our identity in this local neighborhood. "Colonial" and "neogothic" and "functional" had very little to do with who we were. We were not a set of blueprints.

Our denominational supervisor was not happy with our decision to reject the "expert" (his term) counsel he had provided for us. He warned us that we were being very foolish. I think he even used the word "headstrong." He had been through this process dozens of times; we knew nothing. Which was not quite true—we knew nothing about blueprints, but week after week for three years we had been accumulating a sense of church.

One of our building committee members knew of a young architect who had recently begun his practice in our town. I was sent to talk to him. He had never designed a church, but was very interested in what we were doing. He agreed to come and talk with us. A lot of questions were asked back and forth. We liked one another. We asked him to be our architect.

For the next two years Gerry Baxter and his wife worshiped every week with us in our basement, cement-block sanctuary. While leaving worship one Sunday, one of our congregation's teenagers exclaimed to me, "I feel just like one of the early Christians in the catacombs!" She was overheard by her friends. Soon the youth in the congregation had named our church: "Catacombs Presbyterian." The congregation liked it. I liked it. The name never got placed on a sign or printed on our stationery, but it seemed to authenticate noble and sturdy beginnings that reached back to our early church ancestors.

Meanwhile, Gerry Baxter and I had long conversations in which we discussed the formation of a congregation, and I immersed our new architect in all the liturgy I knew. From his side he taught me the aesthetics of space and the way color and light and material textures worked together, the "fit" of the structure with the landscape and the community that would inhabit it. The worship and conversations of that year developed into blueprints, and then a building came out of who we were as we were being formed into a church, a place of worship and learning and community formation. It was simple and honest and beautiful.

While all of this was going on—conversations with our architect Gerry Baxter, discussions with our building committee, getting a feel for the kind of people we were becoming as a congregation—I realized that I was dealing with an artist. I had always assumed that architects designed buildings and that was it. This one understood architecture as an art form in the use of space.

When I had set out to develop this new congregation, I had taken on Moses of the exodus as my mentor. The exodus world is packed with drama featuring charismatic Moses on center stage: his rescue as an infant from the river, the voice from the burning bush, the ten plagues, the Red Sea deliverance, thunder and lightning from Sinai, the Ten Words.

Moses—leading his people out of Egypt into a life of free salvation and forming them into a congregation. Moses—developing a sense of community that was held together by the providence of God, a people who understood themselves in terms of the revelation and action of God. Moses—leading a people into an understanding and practice of being a people of God, a church.

This was new for me. I was in on the ground floor rethinking, reliving the basics—God's salvation, God's revelation, God's community—with variously informed and uninformed people. This was new territory for many in my infant congregation. It was not exactly the wilderness it had been for the people to whom Moses was pastor, for we all had running water in our homes and Safeway bread on our tables. But all of us had the opportunity to rethink and refresh our memories of just what being a people of God consisted of. The life and words of Moses gave us common ground to work from. I wanted to take advantage of this once-in-a-lifetime (for most of us) opportunity to work through the ways in which we lived theology and ethics and worship.

For Moses and his congregation, all the basic stuff of salvation was packed into a story that covered about three months. But the three months in which salvation had been accomplished and revelation defined was just the beginning. A foundation was established, but after four hundred years of Egyptian slavery, this was a lot to take in. This was going to take a while. Forty years, for a start: salvation, the God-shaped life, absorbed—*assimilated*—into their lives?

And then one day during those early years when I was imagining and praying myself into Moses's leadership of his exodus congregation, I discovered Bezalel, and noticed the parallel between what Bezalel did with Moses and his congregation and what Gerry Baxter was doing with me and my congregation.

There are forty chapters in Exodus. I had never read, really read, past chapter 34. Those first thirty-four chapters are where all the action is. At chapter 35, the action comes to a stop. Moses starts talking about Sabbath keeping—what we *don't* do. The first thirty-four chapters narrate the defining actions of salvation and revelation. The final six chapters narrate the preparations for the continuing worship that would assimilate that salvation and revelation into the fabric of their common life week after week, month after month, year after year after year, for another thousand years, at which time Jesus would bring it all to a new beginning. It is here, at chapter 35, that the name Bezalel appears for the first time—Bezalel the artist.

I had never noticed this transition before: the transition from getting the Hebrews involved in the saving and revealing action of God to preparing them for a lifetime of living in response to and participation in that salvation and revelation.

The story of the Red Sea and Sinai, with Moses playing a leading role, defined the life of God's people. Telling and retelling that story in a place of worship would keep their identity alive. With Bezalel playing a leading role, the account of planning, designing, and constructing a building for worship provided a form for rehearsing and practicing their identity in the materials and circumstances of their lives for as long as they lived.

Moses dominates the story during its inception and formation. Bezalel is the architect of its continuation and maturation. At chapter 35, Moses steps aside and hands things over to Bezalel. Bezalel provides the people with the material means for worshiping through the wilderness and living in the promised land, assimilating what had been given at the Red Sea and Sinai. For these final six chapters, Bezalel is in charge. And what he is in charge of is making provisions for worship.

Bezalel is an artist. He is put in charge of designing and preparing and constructing a place of worship that the people could take with them through the wilderness, a portable shrine that they could carry with them and assemble wherever they happened to be. Bezalel designed and supervised the building of the wilderness tabernacle, the portable sanctuary in which the people of Israel worshiped God during their forty years (the approximate half century from 1250 to 1200 BC) of transition from Egyptian slavery to the promised land in Canaan.

And Bezalel goes to work. He designs and oversees the construction of the sanctuary, also called the Tent of Meeting. Meticulous attention is given to every detail that goes into the sanctuary, where every aspect of life is integrated into responsive obedience and a life of salvation: weaving the curtains and covering with careful attention given to fabric, size, design, colors, and embroidery work, along with the hooks and clasps to connect them. Tent poles ("frames") and rods to hold the curtains. Furniture to provide tangible and visual witness to what they are doing: the ark of the covenant, a table for offerings with plates and dishes, bowls, and flagons. An elaborate lampstand with six branches, all of gold. An altar of incense. Holy anointing oil. The Altar of Burnt Offering. Vestments for the priests: robes and tunics, some of them trimmed with bells, a turban crown. A huge work crew. Building materials: acacia wood, skins, gold, silver, bronze, gemstones, cords, pegs.

Worship has to do with a God whom no one has ever seen: "Let us worship God" is our standard rubric. But worship has to do simultaneously with all the stuff we see wherever we look: acacia wood, fabrics and skins, tent pegs and altars, tables and flagons. And this is to say nothing of all the workers in textiles, metal, and wood, weaving and smelting and casting.

First salvation, then worship. First the great events at the Red Sea and Sinai, then bringing every detail and all the stuff of our lives into the sanctuary, where we are formed into salvation, detail by detail, day by day.

To be quite honest, up until that time I had considered worship as something that provided a setting for proclamation and teaching—primarily verbal acts. Now I was beginning to understand it as the formation of salvation, detail by detail, day by day, in the bodies of men and women and babies, neighborhoods, homes, and workplaces, through the "hopes and fears of all the years." The "land of the living" was being created in the place of the land of Egyptian slavery.

Moses led people to salvation freedom; Bezalel paid scrupulous attention to the details of that freedom embodied in

95

a holy life. Moses brought down the Ten Words from Sinai; Bezalel assembled them coherently in acts of offering and sacrifice. Moses *and* Bezalel.

Moses at the Red Sea and Sinai: the once-for-all events of salvation, the story that we keep telling one another to remember who God is and who we are. Bezalel and the Tent of Meeting: the place of worship where a life of salvation identity is formed in time and place, in everydayness and in detail.

Moses the prophet formed my pastoral vocation kerygmatically. Bezalel the artist formed my pastoral vocation liturgically.

Without Moses, worship would soon degenerate into aesthetics and entertainment. Without Bezalel, salvation would fragment into isolation and individualized fits and starts.

An artist, Bezalel, sculpted the piece of art that centered Israel's worship of Yahweh, who cannot be seen or touched, and before whom we can only stand in attentive presence, in prayer and submission, in adoration and obedience. It was an artist who understood that worship had to do with practicing a way of life that was immersed in the salvation and revelation of Yahweh. He led the people Moses had led out of Egypt into making and worshiping in a sanctuary, a place designed to keep them aware and responsive to a way of life in which all their senses were brought into a living participation with the stuff of creation and the energies of salvation. He designed a worship center, the Ark of the Covenant, in which all visibilities converged into an invisibility—Yahweh, a presence, a relationship, who can only be worshiped and never used.[1]

An artist, Gerry Baxter, not only guided my congregation and me in designing and building a church that provided space for telling the story of salvation and revelation, but made sure that everything was ready for a lifetime of worship so that we would understand space not as an emptiness to be filled, but as a fullness to be received. His artistry was responsible for getting us in touch with Bezalel, the artist who developed the forms for a comprehensive sense of worship that formed our understanding of ourselves as ancestors of the people of God into lives of maturing holiness.

Gerry Baxter was my Bezalel. As those months of planning and decision making developed, we worked out in detail what worship required in order to stay connected with our defining story and make adequate provision for its continuous development in the lives of our congregation. The longer we worked together, the more Bezalel came alive for me.

Artists do that. Pastors need artists.

Judith

She entered the sanctuary five minutes or so after I had called the congregation to worship. We were all standing, singing a hymn. She found a place on a back pew. Before the benediction—we were again standing and singing a hymn—she slipped out a side door.

As unobtrusively as she had entered and then left, it was impossible not to notice her. She was about forty years old, slim, and of medium height. Her hair was long, loose on her shoulders, and tinged with gray. Her face was pleasing and open—not beautiful in a classic sense but attractive and generous. No jewelry or makeup. Her clothing matched her appearance: earth-colored, plain blouse, long skirt, denim vest. A vestigial flower child from the sixties and seventies.

She returned every Sunday but preserved her anonymity. After about two months, she stayed for the benediction for the first time and left by the front door where I was greeting the people. She said, "I feel so lucky—I've never heard that story before. I feel so lucky."

That was the Sunday I began a series of thirteen sermons on the life of David. As she left each Sunday, she would often speak some variation on the words I had first heard from her: "I feel so lucky . . . I've never heard that story before."

I still had no idea of who she was. And then after another six weeks or so, she called me on the telephone and asked if she could see me. We arranged for time. She came to my study and told me her story.

She was an artist. She had never been to church before. Never. Her parents were lapsed Quakers—moral, ethical, good. Deeply spiritual people, she thought, but churchgoing and Bible reading were not part of their lives. She lived with an alcoholic husband and a drug-addicted son, and had come to church at the invitation of some friends from her Alcoholics Anonymous meetings who were members of my congregation. And then she said it again, the first words that I had heard from her several months earlier: "I feel so lucky . . . I never knew there were places like this, never knew there were stories like this . . . I feel so lucky."

She was apologetic about being cautious for so long about her identity in the world of artists in which she lived. God and Bible, Jesus and church, were off-color words. They weren't used in polite company. But now she was ready to know more.

So we met together every month or so for conversation. I became her pastor. I listened to her story as it changed in the telling. As we prayed and talked together, she found herself in the large world of salvation and in the presence of Jesus. New dimensions kept opening up. New responses kept developing.

As I became her pastor, she became my personal artist-in-residence. She saw everything as if for the first time, things I had looked at for so long that I had quit seeing them. She heard words with the surprised recognition she named as "lucky," words that had eroded into tired clichés for me. She did for me what artists do: saw the unseen in the seen, heard the no-longer-heard in the heard. She perceived forms and relations in what had become disjointed, broken into fragments by inattention.

Meanwhile her primary community continued to be made up of artists—painters and sculptors and poets—with a few of her twelve-step friends sprinkled among them. She herself worked primarily in textiles. Most of the time she began her work with raw cotton or wool. She made cards, spun dyes, and then wove her fabrics. She made her living by repairing tapestries in museums.

After four years or so of our acquaintance, I moved across the continent to take up a new assignment. Letters replaced conversations. The following is a portion of a letter that reflects the contrasts in her life that developed as she began to live the Christian life.

Dear Pastor: Among my artist friends I feel so defensive about my life—I mean about going to church. They have no idea what I am doing and act bewildered. So I try to be unobtrusive about it. But as my church takes on more and more importance—it is essential now to my survival—it is hard to shield it from my friends. I feel protective of it, not wanting it to be dismissed or minimized or trivialized. It is like I am trying to protect it from profanation or sacrilege. But it is so strong now; it is increasingly difficult to keep it quiet. It is not as if I am ashamed or embarrassed—I just don't want it belittled.

A long-time secular friend, and a superb artist, just the other day was appalled: "What is this that I hear about you going to church?" Another found out that I was going on a three-week mission trip to Haiti and was incredulous: "You, Judith, *you* going to Haiti with a church group! What has gotten into you?" I don't feel strong enough to defend my actions. My friends would accept me far more readily if they found that I was in some bizarre cult involving exotic and strange activities like black magic or experiments with levitation. But going to church is branded with a terrible ordinariness.

But that is what endears it to me, both church and the twelve-step programs, this facade of ordinariness. When you pull back the veil of ordinariness, you find the most extraordinary life behind it. But I feel isolated and inadequate to explain to my husband and close friends—even myself!—what it is. It's as if I would have to undress before them. Maybe if I was willing to do that they would not dare disdain me. More likely they would just pity me. As it is they just adjust their neckties a little tighter.

I am feeling raw and vulnerable and something of a fool. I guess I don't feel too badly about being a fool within the context of the secular world. From the way they look at me, I don't have much to show for my new life. I can't point to a life mended. Many of the sorrows and difficulties seem mended for a time only to bust open again. But to tell you the truth, I haven't been on medication since June and for that I feel grateful.

When I try to explain myself to these friends I feel as if I am suspended in a hang glider between the material and the immaterial, casting a shadow down far below, and they say, "See—it's nothing but shadow work." Perhaps it takes a fool to savor the joy of shadow work, the shadow cast as I am attending to the unknown, the unpaid, the freely given.

Judith the artist working in textiles is an artist still, an artist working in the Christian life. She knows she can't defend or explain it to the satisfaction of her friends. Nobody has any idea what she is doing. She feels apologetic about that, but she embraces what she is given—that seemingly fragile hang-glider life in a Christian community, suspended in mystery, the unknown, the unpaid for, the freely given. She doesn't expect to find nice people, people of accomplishment, artists. But she is an artist of church: "Don't look at me—see the shadow down there. Look at the shadow work. You might see what God is doing."

She brought what Buddhists call the "beginner mind" to this newly discovered world of Jesus and salvation and church. Artists do that. Everyone needs artists. Pastors especially— and especially *this* pastor—need them, for we spend our lives immersed in forms of glory, in the world of salvation become incarnate in Jesus. If because of overfamiliarity and too much talking *about* we no longer see the glory contained in the form, no longer touch the salvation in the body and blood of Jesus, we are no longer pastors.

I want to tell all my pastor colleagues, "Make friends with the artist. Let him rip off the veils of habit that obscure the beauty of Christ in the faces we look at day after day. Let her restore color and texture and smell to the salvation that has become disembodied in a fog of abstraction."

For Further Reading

Hans Urs von Balthasar, *Seeing the Form*, vol. 1 of *The Glory of the Lord: A Theological Aesthetics* (San Francisco: Ignatius Press, 1989)

Martin Buber, *I and Thou*, trans. Walter Kaufmann (New York: Free Press, 1971)

David Bentley Hart, *The Beauty of the Infinite: The Aesthetics of Christian Truth* (Grand Rapids: Eerdmans, 2004)

Calvin Seerveld, *Rainbows for a Fallen World: Aesthetic Life and Artistic Task* (Toronto: Tuppence Press, 1980)

George Steiner, *Real Presences* (Chicago: University of Chicago Press, 1991)

Samantha Wedelich, "There is a river in your heart, what dreams issue forth on those melancholy waves!" Ink on bristol paper.

The Artist

What Exactly Is an Artist, and How Do We Shepherd Them?

BARBARA NICOLOSI

I am not a theologian. I'm not a scholar. I'm actually not an Evangelical, although I have come to consider myself an evangelical Catholic. I am a journalist, a media critic, and serious enough about screenwriting to identify myself as an artist. But I am also somebody who has lived and worked with hundreds of artists for many years. I produced award-winning theater at a small company in Hollywood. And I've spent the last ten years founding a program in Hollywood we call Act One, which trains Christians who want to work as entertainment writers and executives in the mainstream culture. As with anyone else who works shepherding artists, this means I have also, at any given time, had to be a psychologist, pastor, teacher, cheerleader, mentor, mother, policeman, litigator, and, always, friend.

But whatever else I am, I am hopefully always trying to be *alter Christus*—another Christ who intercedes for my artists to the Father.

I love artists and creative people. They make me crazy, but they're rarely boring. When they do get boring, it's because they are working on something they are so passionate about that they become obsessive. An artist caught up in an idea is like an eighteen-wheeler stuck in the sand, just grinding its wheels over and over. It can go on for months! But even when they are boring this way, it is fascinating because being passionate and obsessive is still an intense way of being alive and present to the beauty and complexity of life. When you're around artists, you are around people who are definitely living life to the fullest. Even their despair is gritty and real and fully committed, and I always feel like I'm living that line from the transfiguration scene in the Gospel: "How good it is for us to be here!"

It's amazing to me that when God sends a gift of artistic genius, he usually sends at least one person who *gets* that genius. Genius is always remarkable for freaking most people out. It's one of the marks of genius that it has a prophetic, "this is new and shocking" kind of quality to it. But there's almost always at least one person who's been sent along with the artist to say, "This is amazing!" Vincent van Gogh had his brother, Theo. Emily Dickinson had her sister-in-law, Susan Gilbert. The Beatles had Brian Epstein. When you look at the history of art, you see this person over and over: a certain somebody who was given this gift to save a particular artist for the rest of us. So that might be you, and if it is, I encourage you to take that vocation seriously. There are two kinds of people in the world: people who are artists and people who are supposed to support them. Figure out which you are and do it with vigor.

Who, Really, Is an Artist?

It's hip at the moment to support the arts in the church. I know in L.A. a lot of the churches are conducting arts and drama ministries, and other things like them. The problem, it seems to me, is that we aren't really sure who is an artist in the sense of someone whom we want to support for the general edification of the body of Christ and for the world. There are lots of people doing creative things in the church whose work in the arts seems to me to be much more about their own spiritual or emotional catharsis. The art that they're doing is *for them*, for their own healing. But they don't have divinely-gifted talent.

In one sense, of course, every human being is supposed to be an artist. In his *Letter to Artists*, Pope John Paul II noted that everyone is engaged in crafting the crucial masterpiece of their own life. On another level, in his book *Only the Lover Sings*, philosopher Josef Pieper makes the case that the modern world is so loud and glaring and intrusive that we're losing the ability to see minutely.[1] So every one of us has to become an artist because the practice of art makes us focus on the details. Whether it's gardening, or cooking, or needlepoint, or whatever it is that you do, everyone has to master the details of a craft in order to keep their life vibrant and their perception of God in the "tiny whispering sound" keen.

But in this essay I'm talking about the usual sense of artist, that is, of the talented person called to be prophet and priest for the masses, to edify us in great numbers by the beauty that they are able to bring forth. We need help to figure out who's who because these days every pastor is freaked out over what to do with anyone who walks up to them and says, "I'm an artist, give me money or a microphone or a wall to paint on! You're not going to shut down the Holy Spirit, now, are you?" How should we respond to these folks? How do we properly shepherd the artists in our communities? How do we identify them and learn to release them into their manifold callings? A right understanding of these questions, it seems to me, will lead us to a great vitality in the church.

The Nature of the Beautiful

As a precursor to answering this question, I want to lay out a few ideas about the nature of the beautiful, because *beauty is the terrain of real artists, and one way to recognize them is if they dwell in this terrain.*

Polish philosopher, writer, and actor Karol Wojtyla, who later went by the name Pope John Paul II, spoke about the call of some to pursue what he called "new epiphanies of beauty."[2] This word *epiphanies* here means a kind of ongoing divine illumination in which God cooperates with artists to speak to the world. When an artist pursues the beautiful, he or she opens a channel of revelation between God and humanity. It's an extension of the revelation that occurs through the beauty of creation, about which St. Paul claimed, "For since the creation of the world His invisible attributes, His eternal power and divine nature, have been clearly seen, being understood through what has been made" (Rom. 1:20 NASB).

The nature of beauty

Thomas Aquinas gave a definition of the beautiful that is still helpful and relevant seven centuries later. The beautiful, he said, is wholeness, harmony, and radiance.[3] These define the terrain of the artist.

WHOLENESS

Wholeness means nothing is missing. All parts are present, suggesting completeness. No one looks at the *Pietà* and says, "You know, Mary needs just a little more fringe around her veil. Oh well." Or, people don't listen to Mozart's *Ave*

106

Verum and say, "Needs another high G in there. Oh well." There's something about these works that suggest completeness. Wholeness also means there is nothing extra, nothing gratuitous that isn't an essential part of the whole. Isn't that one of the primary complaints about so many movies? "Gratuitous sex and violence." That is, too often there is no context for these things in a project, so it feels to the audience like they were just slapped in there to try and distract from some flaw in the storytelling. A beautiful work has nothing gratuitous.

And what do we get from wholeness? We are all creatures who have been cut off from our source. There is always a partial emptiness, a longing that can only be filled by divine love. As St. Augustine wrote in his *Confessions*, "You have made us for yourself, O God, and our heart is restless until it rests in you."[4] We yearn to cleave to the One, and when we experience completeness, we have a sense of being at home and at rest. So the beautiful gives us a sense of peace.

HARMONY

Harmony means that all of those parts that are present are related to one another in a complementary relationship. Every part brings out the best in all of the other parts, and there is no domination or submission. And what do we get from harmony? When we experience harmony, we feel a sense of joy, because we are created to dwell in community. We were made by a Triune God whose nature is communitarian, and our destiny is to dwell with him one day in a perfect unity in which every being's full perfection will be manifest. So the beautiful as harmony gives us a joyful taste of this.

RADIANCE

Finally, there's radiance. When we experience a beautiful object, it communicates something profound to us, some kind of moral, spiritual, or intellectual enlightenment. Very often, the communication is beyond language. The subtext of the enlightenment is that the recognition of the beautiful reveals to us our unique dignity as a human person. When you encounter the beautiful, you experience it calling to you personally.

Catholic theologian Cardinal Joseph Ratzinger, now Pope Benedict XVI, has noted that one of the ways you know you have encountered the beautiful is that it feels like personal communication. He notes that the word *beauty* comes from the Greek word *kalen*, meaning "call," because in the moment of the experience of beauty we feel that the revelation has our name stamped on it. Isn't this why we fall in love with artists and musicians whose work has touched us? You want to meet the artist because it feels as though he or she said something to you personally.

We experience our unique human nature every time something inside us responds to something beautiful outside of us. Being able to recognize beauty isn't something that any other kind of creature can do. So the beautiful as radiance gives us an experience of our destiny.

In summary, the beautiful gives us a sense of rest, of joy, and of destiny. No wonder we like it. No wonder it is good for us. But it gets even better.

An experience of the beautiful always involves a paradoxical mix of humility and euphoria. It makes us feel humble because we have the sense that we have stumbled on something completely separate from us, something that existed before us and will go on without us. At the same time, we feel a surge of happiness that we have been personally chosen to be a witness to the beautiful thing. Think of it. I'm standing in front of a beautiful vista, and I say, "Look at the beauty of it. How big and majestic are the cosmos! And how small and insignificant am I, and yet I am so glad I get to see this thing!"

This actually subverts the problem of the Garden of Eden. Satan's temptation was, "You shall be like *gods*." Adam and Eve rejected their creaturehood. And this is the perennial temptation for us: we want to be like God, we want no limits. But the beautiful makes us content in our creaturehood: "I'm small, and that's okay."

As human society has become less agrarian, there is a greater need for the arts to reflect the beautiful to people in our world. My Sicilian ancestors stood at the base of Mount Aetna stomping the grapes and looking out over the crystal blue Mediterranean just beyond the green cliffs, and their spirits would echo back with a prayer of praise: "How good all of this is!" They experienced God in this unmediated creation. The fact that you and I do not have the same access to nature means that there is a greater burden on the church to patronize beautiful art that will make us okay with our creaturehood so that we, too, can feel a yearning to praise swell in our spirits.

What beauty is not

Before I move on, I want to state unequivocally what the beautiful is not. It's not cute. It's not easy. It's not banal. It's not silly. The beautiful is not sweet or nice. It's not facile. And it's not unthreatening. Precious Moments figurines may soothe some kind of deep-seated psychic loss of childhood in people whose parents weren't there for them, or for whom there is a need to oversentimentalize and extend into adulthood the innocence of childhood. But that just means that Precious Moments belongs in a therapist's lobby, not in the church. Could there be anything as horrifically *un*whole as the Precious Moments cross?

So let's be careful what we call beautiful. Call a thing sweet, call it precious, call it pretty. That's fine. There's a place for that. But don't *settle* for pretty or precious when you have something as magnificently glorious as beauty calling out to you.

The Nature of Art

Which brings us to the question: *What is art for?* Now, strictly speaking, the definition of art is that it isn't "for" anything. It is useless—except as *a vehicle of the beautiful*. It's gratuitous. (Of course, as we said before, it is gratuitous without having anything gratuitous!) So why do we do it? Because we human beings are driven to it in a natural response to the cosmos. When we consider our lives and the world, our human nature kicks in and gets our hearts swelling, and we make things to express the resulting ineffable emotions. Every generation is called to do this: to respond to the cosmos of our Triune God with a lasting act of thanksgiving that will be a gift over which future generations can brood and be challenged and know they aren't alone.

When you look at the great cathedrals in Europe, for example, they absolutely accomplish this. I remember bringing a friend from Hollywood to St. Peter's Basilica in Rome. She'd just become a Christian a few years before and had never made it over there. So we walked into the front of St. Peter's at four o'clock in the afternoon, when the rays were coming down through the stained glass—it is stunning at any time of day, but at that time of day it is overwhelming. I had been there several times, and I was thinking as I walked in, "Yeah, this is kind of cool," when suddenly I became aware that my friend wasn't next to me anymore. I found her—this Hollywood screenwriter—standing in the doorway, crying. She said to me, "I'm never going to argue with anyone else about Christianity 'til they've been here." There was something about the beauty of the place that, for her, was proof that humanity and God are everything the church says they are.

What art is not

Tragically, in recent years we've made the arts something else. We've lost the value of just making a sign of praise back to God and his magnificent cosmos. Instead of it just being enough that their work be beautiful, we tell artists that they have to make it do or be other things.

POLITICAL

The first thing we've done to wreck art is make it serve the political instead of the beautiful. I don't necessarily mean left or right, but statement making, which is an utter perversion of the concept of radiance. The goal of statement making is to manipulate, to coerce, to get people to vote a certain way, to propagandize, to merely change behavior.

I can't think of a better example of this than in the awful statue of Mary that stands over the outside door of the $200 million Cathedral of Our Lady of the Angels in Los Angeles. It's just dreadful. The statue is of completely uncertain gender, with a female torso, but harshly cropped hair and distinctly masculine arms and hands. In fact, my students call her "Man-hands Mary." But it's worse than just androgyny. The image has black lips, Asian eyes, a Latino face, and other scattered Anglo features. When I first went on a tour of the new Cathedral, our guide said, "This statue was conceived so that people of all races would see themselves in it and feel welcome in this place." And *I* said, "But it's kind of ugly. I don't know about you, but if you saw that kind of freak inviting you into its house . . ." Well, the tour guide sniffed at me, waved her hand, and said, "The church is not about *that* anymore." It begs the question of whether Japanese people really do look at the *Pietà* in Rome and shrug, "Well, that's okay for the white people."

My point is that the goal of the statue was not to make something that would deliver the beautiful. The goal of the statue was to communicate a political message. The fact that it is ugly and makes my students mock it indicates that it has been a failure as a political vehicle too. In politics, you lose wholeness because the political only tells its own side of the story. As a result, people lose a feeling of rest.

EGALITARIAN

Secondly, we've wrecked art by making it a tool of a sort of egalitarianism, in which we now consider the arts as something that is about making people have better self-esteem.

111

There is an interesting ratio that goes with this egalitarianism: the increase of self-esteem in the untalented people who get to perform stands in direct proportion to the flaying of the aesthetic sensibilities of a thousand others who have to listen to them. What we've done here is to say, "You know what? Doris and Stan have good hearts, and they love the Lord, and they wrote a song." So we let Doris and Stan sing, despite the fact that they have terrible voices. We're not doing it to raise a beautiful song to the heavens. We're doing it to make Doris and Stan feel good.

Somebody needs to say to the pastors who are making the rest of us suffer for Doris's and Stan's self-esteem, "There are *other* ways to make Doris and Stan feel good. It is profoundly unfair to make them feel great but leave me sitting there suffering through bad art."

When we use the arts as a vehicle to make people feel good about themselves, we lose harmony because the relationship of the parts in the piece is now not about perfection or completion, but about suppressing some parts of perfection so that we can have a safe sameness. Recall Salieri's line from *Amadeus*: "I am the patron saint of mediocrity." We've got a lot of those in the church today. Mediocre, unharmonious work lacks the ability to give people the experience of joy.

A SOOTHING DISTRACTION

The third thing we do to wreck the arts is turn them into a soothing distraction instead of a challenging call. This is the background noise we hear so much in the church—noise that can only be called "sacred muzak." It's the stuff they play on elevators to keep people from feeling claustrophobic. We use the arts a lot in the church to lull people so that they don't get too distressed by their sins and too caught up in that whole embarrassing "zeal for your house consumes me" stuff (Ps. 69:9 NIV).

We can't let them have silence during the collection; they might get restless. And so we've got to fill up the silence with noise: "Put something banal on that wall. Have the kids make a felt banner! Just fill up the space." But when we do this, we suppress radiance—the prophetic voice of the arts—and the work communicates nothing worth hearing.

The terrain of the beautiful

Let's talk about artists now. These are people for whom the beautiful is their terrain, so they are going to be people obsessed with wholeness, harmony, and radiance. These are people who play a uniquely priestly role. In his *Letter to Artists*, John Paul II wrote about the "priesthood of the artist." He says the artist stands at the head of the people to offer on their behalf a sacrifice of praise. It's a priesthood because, first, they stand before us. We feed them, support them, put them up there, and then they produce a prayer on behalf of all of us that takes the form of making, not speaking.

Second, a priest is the one who offers sacrifice. In the case of the artists, John Paul II noted that the sacrifice is their own bodies, minds, and spirits as they take on the cross of "the demands of art."[5] The paradox is that as the demands of beauty weigh on the artist, the artist becomes "uglier" as his or her work becomes more beautiful. The more dedicated you become to the pursuit of beauty in your craft, the weirder you get—obsessed and isolated and cut off. This is why artists need a loving family, because only a family will put up with helping an artist carry the cross of the demands of beauty.

The third priestly role of the artist is to be a prophetic voice among the people. They make a response to God from us and God gives a gift of revelation back through them. It's as though the artist becomes God's reed to blow beautiful music through.

It is worth noting that a reed is useless unless it has holes punched in it. The voice of God is too much for the human vessel. The artist has to be stretched and punctured and pulled and misshapen so that they can become a vessel of revelation for the rest of us. Most of the hole punching comes through the exertions of the craft. Long hours of practice make you socially inept. The demands of creativity can be humiliating and full of what the Pope calls the "suffering of insufficiency."[6] And then there is the messiness of baring your heart and soul and darkness in the light for everyone else's gawking pleasure. All of these things punch holes in the artist so that God's message can play through them.

How to Recognize the Artists Among You

I've argued that you will recognize artists by the fact that they dwell in the terrain of the beautiful. I've identified the contours of their priestly calling. Now I want to offer you a few visible signs to help you more specifically identify the artists in your community.

First, in my experience, artistic talent shows up early. I'm very leery of forty-eight-year-olds who come to me and say, "I think I'm going to become a writer." I always want to say back to them, "And I think I'm going to have an IQ of 237." It's not about deciding what talent you have. You either have it, or you don't.

I was in my seven-year-old nephew's second-grade class around Christmastime. Looking up on the wall, it was *immediately* obvious to me which of the little blokes had talent because some of the things on the wall looked like blobs and some looked like reindeer. Not only that, but some kids had put the reindeer in a setting with foreground, while others had them frolicking in the snow. That is, some of the kids were already playing with composition.

I asked my little nephew and his two best friends, Matt and Allen, "Who is the best artist in your class?" And they replied with one refrain: "Joey. Joey can draw."

Don't you wish we could do that in the church? Simply accept the self-evident truth that this kid can draw, and that one can sing, and that one is good at dancing? There is something beautiful in the way kids accept the divine economy, which doles out graces and talent so arbitrarily. It's dreadfully uncivil of God to make us grownups so uncomfortable by giving some kids artistic talents and others none at all.

So, if you want to be a patron of the arts, go into the second grade of your local grammar school, find out whoever produced the coolest reindeer, and then patronize that kid. I'm serious. In twenty years, they'll be painting murals on the city hall in downtown San Diego. Or maybe making a heartrending movie.

A second way to recognize a true artist is that their work has emotional power. Now, when we're talking about the fine arts, most of us today are complete Neanderthals. We know what we like, but we rarely know what we are talking about. For example, I hate opera, and so does nearly everyone in my family. With regard to this unquestionably advanced fine art form, we're all barbarians. But my little sister, Valerie, is an opera singer, and the cross of her life is that her family never appreciates anything that she does. We'll drag ourselves to her shows, saying, "Alright, Valerie, I'll go to *Taranella*—or whatever it is." And Valerie will cry in anguish, "*Tarantella! Tarantella!*"

So one day I bought a Cecilia Bartoli CD to impress her. I had heard her on the *Today Show* and her singing seemed very pleasant to me. Well, I popped it in the CD player when my sister came over, and when I came back five minutes later, my sister, the mezzo soprano, was lying facedown on the carpet, listening to the mezzo soprano Cecilia Bartoli. Now, I had listened to that CD a few times, and I liked it, but I had never been reduced to being facedown on the floor. Valerie, because she knows the art form, was hearing something that moved her so much that her legs went out from under her. Fine artwork has definite emotional power to those who take the time to unlock its secrets.

But it is possible for even unlearned folks like most of us to discern emotional power in less complex art forms. In the movie business, there is a phrase in which we say an actor has "it." When you read a writer who makes you laugh and then a few pages later makes you cry, you know you are dealing with some level of talent. It is a singer who touches your heart and makes you feel connected. It is a photograph that awakens you to someone else's suffering. It is a guitar solo that fills you with awe and delight. This is the emotional power I'm talking about.

I read lots and lots of screenplays, and most often I will fold one up after just a few pages and shrug as I think, *There's no magic here.* But then every so often I'll stumble across a writer who spells poorly, uses the wrong format, and sends us a protest letter arguing that they shouldn't have had to fill out an application. But when I read their work I want to cry. And then I want to meet them. Emotional power is a hallmark of a true artist.

Third, a real artist's work is going to have freshness, a startling quality of something new. I once took a watercolor class. And even knowing very little about composition, I could go down the whole line of student paintings and think to myself, "Derivative, derivative, competent, derivative, competent, derivative . . . Wow! Fresh! It feels like this girl is doing something different." We use this word *freshness* in Hollywood all the time, and it most often connotes a sense of prophecy. When it's fresh, you're hearing a story you haven't heard before quite this way. You're receiving a gift you haven't been given before.

Here's a fourth and final sign of an artist: Artists are obsessed with details of form. This is a God-given preoccupation that marks the sacred gift. Painters are obsessed with matters of brushstroke, canvas size, color, and the relationship of space to objects. Poets worry about meter and meaning, and they are obsessed with words. People have written that they remembered Emily Dickinson as the little girl who used to sit in the corner reading from *Webster's Dictionary* like it was a romance novel.

116

It's worth saying that, for Emily, there was certainly a kind of romance between the poet and the word.

Directors want to know about capturing shadows on film and the minute emotional implications of adjusting a camera lens. Actors want to know what jealousy looks like in a fifty-seven-year-old, repressed, type-A college professor. These details are all minor, but artists care obsessively about them and tend to seek out the company of other people who share their obsessions.

The poet William Butler Yeats observed,

> Does not all art come when a nature, that never ceases to judge itself, exhausts personal emotion so completely that something impersonal, something that has nothing to do with action or desire, suddenly starts into its place, something which is as unforeseen, as completely organized, even as unique, as the images that pass before the mind between sleeping and waking?[7]

In other words, the artist, in learning her craft, has been self-criticizing so much and focusing on these details that she finally gets to a point where the craft is not something she even has to think about. That's when something takes over. It's almost like a trance. Most people I know who tell me they want to be writers, or actors, or anything—they don't *get there*. They're just not that disciplined in their self-criticism.

Two Final Questions

Here are two final questions about artists that may help you make sense of their *modus vivendi*, the way they live out their calling.

The first question is: *Are artists in fact crazy?* I know we've made a lot of jokes at artists' expense, but the question is out there. And sometimes they take advantage of the fact that we think they are crazy by wearing pajamas for three days in a row, right? I'm ashamed to say I've done that. Sometimes it will be two o'clock in the afternoon and I'll still be in my pajamas because I rolled out of bed and started writing. It becomes embarrassing when the UPS guy comes to the door. That's when you might think about throwing on a robe and trying to make your voice sound like you have a really bad cold. But you don't. You're a professional writer.

It does seem that there is a sort of near insanity that comes with the territory of having a creative nature. Emily Dickinson said it this way (paraphrasing here): It's not that the poet sees weird things. It's that other people don't see what's really there.

Another way to look at it would be this: Are there angels in this room? How about the spirits of the saints? And are some of you walking around with demons wrapped like serpents around your shoulders and hissing in your ear?

Now, these unseen spiritual realities are real and are probably really here. Suppose some of us can see them—we'll call these "seers" artists. An artist walks by someone who has a demon wrapped like a serpent around their shoulder, licking their ear, and you go up to that artist and say, "Hey, how are you doing?" And the artist responds, with eyes flashing wildly, "How am I *doing*? How am *I* doing?"

Now, who's the weird one here? The person with the serpent who doesn't recognize it, or the artist who has been rendered socially inadequate by the apparition?

Artists genuinely perceive spiritual realities, and then they open up their mouths and speak in metaphor because they don't know how else to get through to the rest of us who are so obtuse.

In his biography of Edgar Allan Poe—cleverly titled *Poe Poe Poe Poe Poe Poe Poe*—Daniel Hoffman writes, "[Poe] is a marked man, one of the Chosen. Chosen to enjoy what others cannot even sense, chosen to suffer what others know not, to love whom he loves in an isolation as complete as that in which he feels suffering and joy." He goes on to say, "Edgar

Poe was both sane and insane, but sane mostly, especially sane when writing his poems, his criticism, and his tales."[8]

Artists are extremely sane when they are working on their projects. These people can be crazy about the details of their noncreative lives, completely unable to mail back their auto insurance payments. But honestly, if you only have twenty-four hours in a day, what's more important?

Yeats has another great line: "When I found my verses too run of the reds and yellows Shelley gathered in Italy, I thought for two days of setting things right . . . by eating little and sleeping upon a board."[9] That's the craziness of the artist. But is that really crazy? Is it weird to sleep on a board so that your writing wouldn't be elaborate and ornamental? That's the kind of thing that would make you say, "He is insane." But is he?

The second question is: *Are artists lazy?* They have the reputation of being lazy because they dread their work. But they dread it because it's very, very hard. And they also get bored once they've figured out what they have to do, and then it is torture to actually have to revisit the whole problem and take it out of their heads and translate it into some kind of form. "I'm actually going to have to do it now?" It's as if the problem has been solved and they've moved on.

I think the other reason they look lazy to nonartists is that the process of art often takes place under the surface. For example, I don't look like it, but right now I'm trying to solve a first-act dilemma in a screenplay I'm writing. I've been working on it for three months. I need to find a choice for a Carmelite nun that will occur at the end of the first act and demonstrate to the audience that she's lost her faith. I can't have her throw a crucifix into the fire because they already did that in *Amadeus*, but that moment I'm trying to find, that choice, is obsessing me. I've been living with it for three months. And to my friends, it doesn't look like I'm accomplishing very much on the project. But they don't know how many bad character choices I've been rejecting all these months. Am I lazy because

I don't have much to show for the last three months? No, it's just hard work to make good art.

In Conclusion

The truth is, we have a long way to go to renew what John Paul II called "that fruitful dialogue that used to exist between the Church and the arts."[10] It's going to be a journey to reconstitute guilds in the church in which we can breed a new generation of artists. It's going to be tough to convince the whole people of God that the arts are a serious and necessary part of what we do as the church. But I have a lot of hope. There are many signs that the Holy Spirit is leading us into a whole new renaissance of the arts in the church.

For those of you who are pastors, I want to encourage you to hang in there with us artists. Artists aren't the easiest breed to shepherd. Like I said, we're crazy, but not always. Many of us have a deep love for God. Many of us love the church, and many of us *want* to love the church and need help to love her. Please be patient. Pray for us. Know that your prayers and pastoring will help us do the work of making beauty manifest. And that, in the form of a Christ-given experience of peace, joy, and destiny, is good for the whole world. As Dostoevsky said, when all else fails, "Beauty will save the world."[11]

For Further Reading

Madeleine L'Engle, *Walking on Water: Reflections on Faith and Art* (New York: Shaw Books, 2001)

Flannery O'Connor, *Mystery and Manners* (New York: Farrar, Straus and Giroux, 1969)

Pope John Paul II, *Letter to Artists* (Chicago: Liturgy Training Publications, 1999)

Josef Pieper, *Only the Lover Sings: Art and Contemplation* (San Francisco: Ignatius, 1990)

Arthur Pontynen, *For the Love of Beauty: Art History and the Moral Foundations of Aesthetic Judgment* (Edison, NJ: Transaction Publishers, 2005)

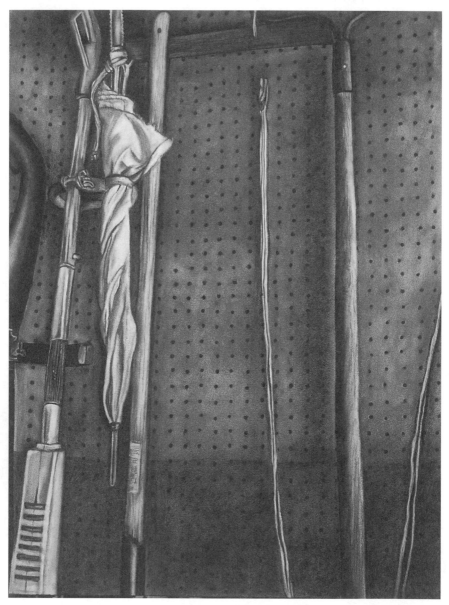

Anita Horton, "Avarex." Charcoal.

The Practitioner

Nurturing Artists in the Local Church

Joshua Banner

I've spent much of my life working beside my father and grandfather in the corn and soybean fields of central Illinois. We had two John Deere tractors, model 4020. These were used to do the bulk of the field work. I sat on the wheel cover next to the square radio that was mounted to the right of the driver. With one hand I gripped the radio to keep my balance. I was ten when my grandfather first told me to slide over and take the enormous wheel. We swerved, bounced, and jostled over the clods of dirt. Grandpa said I was oversteering. Slowly, with his hand placed on mine, I began to understand the subtle nudges the steering wheel needed to keep the tractor headed in a straight line. In keeping with the antiquated idea of *husbandry*, it was through lessons like this that my grandfather showed me that a good farmer is essentially a nurturer. A good farmer loves the land.

Wendell Berry, the poet-farmer, once said, "The standard of the exploiter is efficiency; the standard of the nurturer is care."[1] The nurturer is concerned with *giving to* the land so that it can sustain production. The exploiter is interested in short-term gain and *taking from* the land. Berry acknowledges that both of these impulses are within us. Each of us is both nurturer and exploiter.

There have not been many examples for me to follow as a pastor to artists, so the carefulness of a farmer has become a point of reference for me. Many of us, I recognize, are having to learn by experimentation. In my first ten years of ministry, I often found myself straining and bucking against restraints. The example of a farmer has challenged me to slow down. I need to learn how to take the long view and to keep in mind that the way in which I perceive the ultimate purpose of the arts will affect the way I approach artists, whether I nurture their gifts or exploit them.

Behind the sanctuary at Bridgeway, a church in Oklahoma City where I began as an intern in 1998, there is a long, ridiculous cave of a room where kids chased each other in games of tag after the service or groups gathered for planning sessions. Over time we slowly transformed this room into "The Backroom," with track lighting, handmade paper lanterns, eclectic cast-off sofas and chairs, and a sprawling painting of a tree adding its metaphorical gravitas to the stage. The room became host to art exhibits, music concerts, poetry readings. It became a kind of garden where, willing but unwitting, I became not just an intern but a Pastor of Worship and Art. In this Backroom I did a lot of pastoring of creative people.

Three Artists

Had you wandered into The Backroom at that time, you would have found artists like Justin, Shelly, or Michael.

I met Justin in a church basement when he was leading Cordelia's Rebellion, his high school scream-rock band. Justin, always spiritually hungry, was part of our church for several years. When he returned from rehab, his music took a different turn. Today, almost ten years later, his current band is well known in Oklahoma City. Never quite securing a record deal but still making music that is painfully beautiful, his vocals are urgent, raw, and simple. He is enamored with Alvin Plantinga and philosophy of religion. He hopes a teaching job one day might help him support his wife and daughter.

Shelly grew up in a conservative Church of Christ home. She is softspoken and quite modest. During my first summer in Oklahoma, Shelly and I traveled with several others on a month-long mission trip to Honduras. The whole trip I had no idea she was an art student. That fall I began the small gallery in The Backroom and discovered Shelly's paintings. It didn't take much prodding for her to continue to submit her work throughout college. Some of her classmates came and went from The Backroom, but Shelly remained steady. She finished a degree in Advertising Design. Now she uses ceramic tile to assemble mosaic installations and mixed media wall pieces, each with vibrant, modeled embellishments of nature.

Michael was the first college student to ask me to mentor him. Our friendship developed quickly, with many late-night ramblings about novels and poetry. Michael became one of our best writers. He stood out among the many other student leaders of our campus fellowship groups. During his senior year, old memories of childhood trauma resurfaced and he dropped out of leadership. He stopped going to church and gave up writing poetry for a long season. We continued to share an affection for Thomas Merton. Today, while completing a master's degree in poetry, he navigates between agnosticism and Buddhist meditation techniques. He remains fascinated with Jesus.

The Pastor as Nurturing, Loving Farmer

These relationships have been messy and, at times, unpleasant. I've struggled with patience, expected too much, pushed too far, and overstretched my own small spool of energies. But the use of a gentle, consistent hand is, despite my stumbling, effective. Why? Because the arts are made *by* people *for* people—each as intricate and organic as the corn my grandfather raised. In this very human endeavor, I have to continually remind myself that the arts are not buttons we push to enhance a sermon. They're not levers we switch to intensify an evangelistic tactic. Art has to do with people we love, and this love bears witness to Christ.

What has unfolded for me in my arts ministry will be different than what you discover in yours. But I believe there is something universal about the connections between what I define here as pastoring, promoting, and producing the arts. As farmer-pastors, we are lovers. We tenderly work the soil of our culture by identifying artistic gifts with discernment (pastoring). Then our joyful response to discovering the artists is to push their gifts outward in order to share their creativity with others (promoting). Finally, we prune the gifts and coach the artists to mature so that their fruit will be sustainable and long lasting (producing). We are all learning as we press onward. I pray that what I share here of my journey opens up possibilities for the flourishing of artistic creativity in your community.

To Pastor: A Foundation of Trust

> And when, expecting someone we love, we put a tablecloth on the table and decorate it with candles and flowers, we do this not out of necessity, but out of love.
>
> Alexander Schmemann

I sensed a calling to church work from a young age. My path into ministry was a conventional one. I enrolled at Wheaton

126

College thinking I'd study the Bible and theology. Then I'd go to seminary. I had no intention of rummaging around in the arts. In fact, the art students in my classes intimidated me. There was no one like them among the forty-two people of my high school graduating class in my hometown of Fisher, Illinois—a town with a smaller population than Wheaton's enrollment. I found myself fascinated by these "creative spirits." They had long hair, thrift-store clothes, unshaven faces (men) and legs (women). Some seemed phlegmatic and mysterious. Some appeared flamboyant and uninhibited. One of my classmates wore an ankle-length skirt and walked barefoot through campus in November! Who were these people? How did they come to be so seemingly different?

Artsy. Right-brained. Eccentric. Weird. Strange. Bohemian. Avant-garde.

I hid in the back of my Art Survey course freshman year. I wept through slide after slide of da Vinci, Pollock, Kandinsky, van Gogh, Picasso. They awakened something in my soul. To be sure, it was a visual feast for which my young imagination starved.

But it was a ceramics studio that infected me with a love for the creative process. My professor had carpal tunnel syndrome. The pain in his wrists made it difficult for him to work with the clay of his own sculptures, so the formative work was done by his advanced students—which I was not, but he invited me to help anyway. I was just a maintenance person keeping the clay moist. I spent hours working the surface of the near-finished pieces, cleaning away excess bits of clay and smoothing out the surface with a blue rubber rib. It was an invigorating, exciting, deep, and profound way to spend and share time with others. In the studio we spoke a language I felt I had known but never used.

The fall after graduation, I met with this professor over coffee. He asked, "What's your dream job? What do you really want to do?" My surprising, immediate response was, "To

127

be around creative people." I wanted to share in the waking
life of artists for the remainder of my own.

The power of sharing in the life of an artist

This is the substance of what I hope to do as a pastor of
artists: to draw near to artists and to share in their work. As
in soulful prayer, this sharing results in a resounding, "Amen!
Let it be so!" The physical materials of paint, canvas, clay,
stone, pen and ink, the wood of a guitar or cello, or the stage
or screen mediate a communion among us. Together we become something more than we are as individuals. Our role
as nurturers of the arts, then, is to gather people to share an
experience with art. In our collected participation we offer
the artist an "Amen! Amen!"

This is what artists ache for. Their feelings of loneliness, of
being misunderstood and underappreciated, are not unwar-
ranted. Statistically, only 10 percent of the graduating class
of any given arts degree will still be making art ten years
later. Of that 10 percent, only a tenth of them will be making above a measly $10,000 a year from their work. David
Bayles and Ted Orland aptly describe an artist's self-doubts:
"You're not up to the task . . . you can't do it, or can't do it
well, or can't do it again; or that you're not a real artist, or
not a good artist, or have no talent, or have nothing to say."[2]
Combine alienation with financial challenges, and it is easy
to see why artists struggle with fear.

As an undergraduate, I spent a summer in Chicago doing
outreach work in a rough neighborhood. My roommate and
I read about Mother Teresa and asked for God's heart for
the "unlovely": the homeless, the prostitutes, the dealers.
Ironically, when I returned to Wheaton, I began to see that
the eccentric artists, the very students that intimidated me,
were the unlovely of our college community. They were on
the fringe, the marginalized. Who nurtured their souls? During my senior year, I gathered a group to meet once a week
to talk, read Scripture, and pray. A drummer, a songwriter,

two creative writers, and a sax player—in my dorm room. That was the beginning of my arts ministry.

It was hard at first to know how to share in the lives of these artists. I struggled with my own fears: fears that they wouldn't respect me as an artist or that I'd seem boring or uncool. I grew my hair out and pierced both my ears. I stopped shopping for clothes at the mall. My first attempt at a beard was pathetic, so I shaved it off. I also failed at the messy, bedhead look. My endeavors at bohemia were not so much about art as they were about belonging. So I abandoned my preconceived notion of what it meant to be an artist. I decided to spend more time trying to make good art instead of working so hard to look like an artist.

The importance of intentionally pursuing people

As a pastor, I understand that the initiative to bridge the distance is my responsibility. Artists can be shy and self-effacing, or brusque and unresponsive. More significantly, many have not imagined what a relationship with a church might mean. The arts and the church seemingly exist in different conceptual worlds. In order to break into the world of an artist, all I need is sincere curiosity and interest in sharing in the artist's world.

Rachel was something of a loner. She was acutely independent with a strong personality. I remember watching her stomp to the beat of the worship music in her hiking boots, dreadlocks flying. She enjoyed participating in our worship services, but came only when she felt like it. I met her after leading a Bible study at an apartment near the University of Oklahoma. Something I'd said betrayed my interest in the arts, so she approached me afterward to say hello. Our first conversation began something like this:

What is your medium?
Printmaking? Oh yeah? What kind?
How long have you been making prints?

What subjects interest you?

Which artists are your influences?

What inspires you?

And the most important question:

When do I get to see your work?

I invited myself into her studio space. We met with some of her friends for lunch and then she took me to the art building. She pulled her work out of a locker and let me spend an hour looking over them. Fascinated by her sense of color, I asked to borrow a few pieces. The next time I saw her, she called me her new best friend. In time Rachel became one of my most regularly featured artists.

If an artist doesn't have a concert scheduled soon or a gallery opening, I invite myself into their studio space. Songwriters often have a couple recorded songs they will give me on a disc. Sometimes I invite them to sit down with a guitar to show me a new song in person. With visual artists, I especially like to visit their creative space and see works in progress. Writers email me drafts of this and that. We don't need to be experts in each artist's medium. We simply need to be curious and demonstrate that we believe what artists are doing is important—to call their creative risks "good" just as the Creator blessed his own handiwork in the first seven days—and to bless that work by giving it our attention and sharing in it. If Christians should excel at anything, it is sharing with each other deeply.

Pastoring, I suggest, should be understood as being synonymous with nurturing. All Christians are called to nurture and care for others. Yet those in leadership, pastors and lay leaders, should be distinguished largely because they are capable of extending care to others. A nurturer possesses the initiative necessary to penetrate the outer shell, the crusted topsoil, of a person's life. A nurturer is able to till the soil. A nurturer moves past layers of presumption and self-reliance in order to earn a person's trust so that he will receive love. Each of us will have particular types of artists we are drawn to and who are drawn to us. The question is: How do we earn their trust?

When I moved from Chicago to Oklahoma, I had resigned myself to a vast landscape of strip malls, multiplex cinemas, and college sports rivalries. Yet as a campus ministry intern, I kept meeting artists on each of the college campuses I'd visit. We used our few resources to gather and promote the arts: concerts, poetry readings, literary and photo journals, an art gallery, new paintings, poems, worship songs, dances, whole new records, creative collaborations, songwriting, and creative writing workshops. And we went out into our community with our art to display God's gift of creativity. We moved from being hidden in The Backroom of the church to becoming a substantial dimension of the church's identity.

The art events were important, but the ultimate purpose was to love artists, to draw them out and involve them in the larger fellowship of the congregation. How can the local church serve artists, and how can the artists serve the church? Extending fellowship means *sharing* in their world. You may not think of your town as a hotbed of artistic activity, but you may be surprised to find creativity hidden in the backroom of your church.

In reaching out to artists, I've had the advantage of being one myself. But I don't believe it is necessary for a pastor to be an artist in order to love and serve artists. All you need is the desire to share in their world. You need the willingness to get to know them—to attend to the details of their lives. And you need the patience to let mutual trust develop. More often than not, it will come. And what a beautiful thing that is.

To Promote: Moving the Artist Outward

> It's about two percent movie-making and ninety-eight percent hustling. It's no way to spend a life.
>
> Orson Welles

So, you've established a trusting relationship with an artist and you want to see this artist continue to grow. You've found different ways to share in her world, to celebrate her, and she is encouraged. What more can you do?

The risk of going public

Promoting an artist is a matter of moving her from a private to a public audience. That includes anything from a Sunday morning service to an outdoor concert. The trust we've built as pastor-nurturer with the artist grants us the discernment and the access to identify and release an artist's gifts. Like the farmer, we can take the artist as a seedling and place her out in the soil to grow deep roots and to produce fruit. Of course, definite risk exists in this movement outward. The artist exposes herself to harsher winds, such as the potential for large-scale rejection from fickle critics. She also widens the implications of her creative vision by sharing it with a larger audience. A key reason why artists peter out over a ten-year period is that they have no audience. Some theorists go so far as to claim that a piece of art is only half finished by the artist; the audience finishes the creative process by beholding and interpreting the artwork.

What makes matters more difficult is that most artists also do not know how to go about finding their own audiences. They need managers, advocates, friends, brokers—promoters to give them a shove out onto the stage. When I promote an artist, I am able to make a considerable commitment to her work by investing space and time. It is one thing for me to say that an artist's work is good in private; it is another to join in the risk and thrill of artmaking when I give her a stage. It is immensely encouraging for an artist to hear someone say, "You need to perform that. More people need to see this, hear this, feel this."

I recently heard Rob, a young songwriter, perform the same set of songs at two different music venues. It was such well-written music that I invited him to spend a weekend recording those songs in the college's studio. My goal is not to get Rob on the radio or even to launch him into a music career. My goal is to broaden the opportunity for listeners to gather around him with an "Amen. This is good. This is true." In this way, we water his soul.

The art of discernment

Promoting an artist requires careful discernment. I need to know that an artist's work is prepared for an audience and identify which pieces of art are ready to be shown. We have to exercise a hefty patience here. One of the greatest ways we care for an artist is to release his gifting *slowly* into the public arena. Opportunities to promote an artist will consistently come. It is easy to give an artist a platform; it is difficult to take that platform away. One artist will be shy and need a shove. Another will be overeager and need to be held back, if only to form his character, to show him that we value his person over his talent, his *being* over his *doing*. My rule of thumb is not to promote an artist publicly until he has been involved in the church for a season of time—six months to a year at least. I'm not looking for an artist to have his life perfectly sorted out. I'm emphasizing the call to Christ and discipleship, to form identity first in him instead of his talents.

A high school student named Chris once came to me with a drawing he had done on notebook paper in study hall. He wanted me to display his piece in the church gallery space. I said no, which clearly hurt his feelings. Chris was excited about his drawing and told me the story about how he felt closer to God while being creative. I shared in his excitement, praised him for his hard work, pointed out specific parts of the drawing I found interesting, but remained firm in my decision not to display his piece.

This was a formative opportunity. I explained to Chris that the gallery space was used to promote artists who dem-

133

onstrated a substantial commitment to developing their artistic skills. Advanced artists can go through multiple drafts
and endure constructive, critical feedback from peers in a
workshop, then continue to revise before they have art that is
ready to be shown. I offered to buy Chris some high-quality
paper and some nice, fine-point ink pens. I suggested that I
would consider displaying a more developed, final draft of his
drawing. I sought to encourage him by acknowledging that
what he had started on the notebook paper was an excellent
first draft that needed more work.

This is a delicate role to play in the journey of an artist.
We are helping her to discern her strengths and weaknesses.
Diving into this intimate arena of a person's life is the stuff
of pastoral care. Here we are given a distinct vantage point
into the artist's character, the raw nerve endings of her deepest fears and most profound joys. Some artists will discover
they are not as gifted as they'd hoped. Others may begin to
comprehend the full extent of their talent for the first time.
Our aim is to create a safe place for artists to risk.

It is difficult in our egalitarian society to envision an environment that can both nurture novices as well as celebrate
highly trained excellence, embrace both folk art and fine art.
Surely if there is any place on earth where this can happen,
it is in the body of Christ where love "is not jealous; it does
not brag and is not arrogant. . . . It bears all things, believes
all things, hopes all things, endures all things" (1 Cor. 13:4,
7 NASB). We want to guard against elitism, yet we also do
not want to deny the vital role a faith community can play
to hearten artists who have made a serious commitment to
their respective crafts. The challenge for the local parish is to
promote creativity in all of its diverse potentialities.

Different venues, different purposes

It is useful therefore to have differing creative venues that
correspond to the varying levels of creative ability. For ex-

ample, in the case of the high school student, instead of displaying his notebook drawing in one of the rotating gallery shows, I might hold on to his piece and display it at an annual Spring "Art Expo" where any and all artists have freedom to display their work. Such an exhibition might draw artwork from both children and the elderly. The art expo serves the same function for a visual artist that the "open mic" serves for musicians. Songwriters who are not ready for a full-fledged concert sign up for short, ten- to fifteen-minute sets without an audition. The open mic is a safe place for artists to "cut their teeth." People attend knowing that performers are risking, and therefore the audience is accordingly forgiving and supportive. A free-for-all art expo or an open mic are both good places for churches to begin promoting novice artists.

Beyond the walls of the church

Finally, with respect to promotion: What about the artists whose work does not fit into a corporate worship service? A full, gospel vision for arts ministry is one that attempts to nourish a wide spectrum of the arts, both inside and outside the church building, both within and beyond a Sunday service. If we engage only the so-called liturgical arts, we are modeling an unfortunate dualism that separates Sundays from the rest of the week. We need artists who will work in the church and those who will work in the marketplace.

For the sake of loving and developing advanced artists, seek partnerships with venues in the community at large. Songwriters and poets need to frequent open mics hosted at the local bar and grill, and friends from church need to show up in force to cheer them on. Co-promote concerts with other concert venues. Keep track of community art events and make information available at the church both for the artists and patrons. Writers need to submit their work to journals and contests. Visual artists need to get shows at local restaurants, cafés, and galleries.

This movement outward is motivated by a love for both the artists and the arts. Yet it is further underwritten by the missional calling of the church. These public venues are our harvest fields. We are not only promoting the arts at a public level. We are impelling the church out into the community to be salt and light, a creative witness of the glory of God upon the earth: "This is to my Father's glory, that you bear much fruit, showing yourselves to be my disciples" (John 15:8 NIV).

To Produce: Pruning, Weeding, Cultivating . . . Critiquing

> I work from likes and dislikes, and not by literary logic. Not by words, but by being satisfied with form.
>
> Henry Moore

The art of critique

Now, then, how do we critique and identify art to promote? We serve the artist by lovingly pruning her work, clarifying it, and thus more purposefully launching her onto the stage. By using the term "produce," I intend to improve upon its meaning within the movie and music industries. Producing here is not for the sake of targeting a lucrative market. Producing is a focused and wholly trust-based nurturing of an artist through critique. Honest, loving critique is a rigorous, hands-on engagement, a most effective way to identify and release artistic gifts. Rest assured, you do not need to be an expert in order to learn how to do this well. You simply need the foundation of trust and a careful, gentle hand. Producing may seem intrusive, but, done well, it can be the most explicit way of loving the artist.

You might be tempted to butter up your artists with praise. In the short term, the artist might experience a greater ego boost. But in the long run, he may acquire a false sense of confidence concerning his skills and, consequently, take artistic risks for which he is not ready. Steady, consistent, clear, and honest feedback prepares an artist to succeed.

One of my students recently reminded me how important it is for me to be consistent. Last year I had given Dan a few opportunities to lead songs for our worship services. I've always encouraged him as an excellent musician, but I've had some reservations about the strength of his voice and leadership presence. Partway into this new school year, I began to notice a dark cloud hovering over Dan during our rehearsals. He was irritable and short with me. I returned home after an evening service to find a heated email from him. We met the next day to talk it out, and I realized that I had made a significant mistake. I had not adequately followed up on my critique of Dan's vocal leadership. I'd moved on to promoting other students and he felt confused and forgotten. He began to distrust my words of praise. It wasn't that Dan was afraid of my critical feedback. It was that I hadn't returned consistently over time to that conversation to help him more clearly understand my concerns and find ways to improve upon his weaknesses.

Encouraging words affirm the artist's strengths and make it easier to receive critical feedback. Yet positive feedback without criticism can become insincere. The critical feedback helps the artist put his strengths into perspective. The artist wants to know where he stands in the grand scheme of his development. The criticism at first may seem discouraging, but to the better artists, criticism is a challenge. This criticism has to be steady and dependable in order to gain access into the inner workings of an artist's development.

I rarely offer negative feedback immediately after a performance. At that moment the artist needs love and appreciation. Instead of saying, "Wow! How amazing! You were fantastic!" I'll say, "Thank you so much for sharing with us! Thank you for risking. I'm glad you had this opportunity. How did you feel out there?"

Often, the artist herself will then reveal her own concerns. In fact, after stepping off a stage, the artist may be at her most vulnerable. We don't need to flatter in order to love her at this point. We need to help her turn off her harsh inner editor. "Hold on. You're your own worst critic. Sure, there are things you could improve, but the perfect performance? Friend, it doesn't exist."

It is good for an artist to get some emotional distance from her work before I assess it more objectively. I give it a day or more and, even then, I don't impose my feedback. I need to offer it. In fact, I'll ask the artist before the performance if she wants feedback. That way she can mentally prepare. "What would you like to talk about? What kind of feedback do you want? What do *you* think were your strengths and weaknesses?"

Before I cite any criticism, I need to do everything I can to make sure the artist knows that I did indeed take in the whole of her work. She needs to feel safe and know that I wasn't just hunting for her failures. It is important for me to attempt to identify at least three positive items before addressing anything critical.

A teachable heart

When I get to the point of criticism, I keep in mind that how the artist receives feedback is revealing. In the church we prize a teachable character. Nobody is harder to work with than a diva unwilling to recognize where she might grow and improve. This kind of aloof attitude doesn't only affect my relationship with her; it can negatively affect the entire community. Regular, honest feedback, something each artist should seek out, needs to be a given within a healthy arts community. I model this as a pastor by asking my leaders for regular critique of my music and teaching because I also want to grow. This levels the field by communicating that all of us are in process. There is no one who has "arrived," no one who has nothing left to learn.

138

The art of peer critique

As in all good leadership, one particular necessity is delegation. When a community grows, we won't have the capacity to be as intentional with each and every one of our artists. The workshop (also called peer editing) is a great tool that removes from me the burden to know *everything* about *every art form*. In small groups, ideally composed of eight or fewer people, artists meet regularly to present their work and offer each other constructive criticism. The same rule of thumb applies within these groups: positive responses before critical.

Another prerequisite to abide by: no disclaimers! The artist presenting should have little or no opportunity to explain or defend her work. The art should be received on its own terms. Allow the artist to speak only when the critique is over—and then, only to clarify the feedback she's received. Groups that meet over extended periods of time benefit most from the workshop. It takes time for the members to trust each other and understand the context of each person's criticism. And finally, no one should be forced to agree with the criticism she receives! An artist may incorporate some of the criticism and decline the rest. In the long run, workshops provide an immediate audience and deadlines that hold artists accountable to working intentionally toward completion of their work.

Let me clarify. When producing, we are not pronouncing a distinction between "good" and "bad" art, but between *preparation* and a *lack of preparation* for an audience. In certain cases, you will need to tell an artist the hard truth that it isn't going to work out. Her art will not be used publicly, but you will have walked with the artist far enough and know her work well enough to give her specific reasons why. This, too, is loving.

The art of speaking a hard word

During one season at Bridgeway Church, a group of women had been meeting in The Backroom on Saturday mornings to dance. They had decided among themselves that they were ready to go public. I met with Mindy to discuss their vision to form a dance ministry. The trouble was that I knew nothing about dance. Usually I will ask the artists themselves to teach me about their craft. In this situation I would have liked to have seen the dancers perform elsewhere and to have had some time to talk afterward to learn more about different kinds of dance. The difficulty was that none of these ladies had formal training. Mindy explained that a few of them had been to a worship conference that had inspired them to use their bodies to honor God. Their Saturday mornings had freed them to discover deeper connections with worship. I was excited about her excitement. It seemed that good things were indeed happening, yet I had no way to know if they were ready for a public audience. I needed a tutor, someone whom I could trust both as a worshiper and an experienced dancer.

Several months after dialoging with Mindy, I searched around and met Sky Marie. She was a dance student at the University of Oklahoma who attended a small group within our church. I invited her to choreograph some movements for an Easter service. It was a solo piece that was beautifully executed. Sky began to help me understand the difference between modern dance and classical ballet. In time, we added more dance to our services. I began not only to understand more about dance, but to appreciate and be moved by it as well.

Unfortunately, Mindy was frustrated with me. I didn't see her much after our initial set of conversations. I've learned that some artists will be frustrated with the amount of time required for a church body to be stretched. But it is better to deal with their provocation earlier than later, when it snowballs into deeper puzzlement and more hurt feelings. We love artists by preparing them. If they don't want coaching or to take time to prepare, then, unfortunately, they are most likely not the best people to promote publicly. We are as responsible for discerning the preparedness of a person's character as we are for discerning the preparedness of her gift.

It took a couple years for us to include dance into our worship life. We started by planting small seeds. We learned together more about what fit well. I wanted to take Mindy and the other ladies seriously enough to appropriately introduce dance to our church so that it could substantially take root. Dance is an excellent way to help a body of worshipers understand the physicality of worship, the goodness of our "fearfully and wonderfully made" bodies. It is such an important art form that it deserved to be introduced to our congregation in its best possible manner.

A final area for discernment is how to encourage both beginner and advanced artists. Sometimes it is worth risking a new artistic direction that is underdeveloped. We do need to let our artists be beginners and to let them make mistakes. However, we should always be capable of challenging our artists to offer their best. We need to discern when to push toward excellence and when to be patient. Excellence does glorify God, but our pursuit of excellence should never reduce our artists to being means to an end. We glorify God not just with our final art presentation; we glorify him in the gracious and patient way we engage in the process of artmaking.

It takes tremendous courage and commitment to persist. In nurturing an artist, we as pastors come alongside to encourage, support, and push him further into his work than he might have gone otherwise. Here the cheering on is not a response only to the end result, but to the entire journey.

In Conclusion: The Long View

> Indeed, the whole distinction between art and trash, between food and garbage, depends on the presence or absence of the loving eye.
>
> —Robert Farrar Capon

141

Farmers, pastors, and artists have at least two things in common: patience and process. Farming takes time and results from a great deal of sweat. A farmer has no such thing as a "quick fix." Tools repaired haphazardly soon break again. If we are to nurture the arts, we will need to have the long view in mind, just like a farmer who plants tiny seeds and does not despise small, slow beginnings. Like the farmer, we should be as interested in the labor of planting and working the ground as we are in the harvest.

The greatest gift the arts have to offer us is a lively attentiveness—a wakefulness—to the beautiful and interesting things our Father Creator has surrounded us with. The past five decades of popular culture have produced quite a bit of dehumanizing, banal art. The bleak prospect of what Carl Bernstein has called the "idiot culture" presents exciting opportunities for the gospel to inspire a thoughtful, alternative vision of culture that bears witness to Christ.[3]

How can the gospel find a vibrant witness through the arts to transform our neighborhoods and cities? We must begin with a renewal of our churches before we have anything to offer the culture outside the church. And we begin this renewal not by asking what the arts can do for the church, to vary on John F. Kennedy's dictum, but how the church can serve the arts. As patient, careful stewards, we, as pastors and leaders, can nourish the soil of our culture by the way we love artists intentionally—loving not only their artwork, but who they are as persons in process.

For Further Reading

Jeremy Begbie, *Beholding the Glory: Incarnation through the Arts* (Grand Rapids: Baker Academic, 2001)

Wendell Berry, *The Art of the Commonplace: The Agrarian Essays of Wendell Berry* (Berkeley: Counterpoint, 2003)

Frederick Buechner, *Telling the Truth: The Gospel as Tragedy, Comedy, and Fairy Tale* (New York: HarperOne, 1977)

Eugene H. Peterson, *A Long Obedience in the Same Direction: Discipleship in an Instant Society* (Downers Grove, IL: Inter-Varsity, 2000)

Chaim Potok, *My Name Is Asher Lev* (New York: Anchor, 2003)

Shaun Fox, "Poster series for the International Campaign to Ban Landmines."
Digital illustration.

The Dangers

What Are the Dangers of Artmaking in the Church?

W. David O. Taylor

Art is a task like building bridges and fixing meals, it takes intelligence, sensitivity to needs, and specialized knowledge.

Calvin Seerveld

For some of us, asking about the dangers of art is like asking "What are the dangers of the rocket ship?" when we've
only just figured out how to make a wheel. Why focus on the
negative consequences of art when we struggle to introduce
the meagerest of art into our services? When Augustine tells
us that instrumental music is for weak souls and Calvin de-
clares that "even if the use of images contained nothing evil,
it still has no value for teaching," why stop for an extended
investigation of dangers that, for most of us, are abstract?[1]
The concern, I recognize, is fair.

But naming the dangers is part of our growing up. It is what it means to mature. We have no business remaining naïve or impulsively enthusiastic, as if all we needed were merely *more* art. Rather, we need good art that serves the good purposes of the church. And that requires a great deal of wisdom and humility.

In this chapter I want to map out a landscape of some dangers that we will encounter as we increase the amount, intensity, and diversity of artistic activity in our churches. This landscape will include the following topographical features: one personal anecdote, two big ideas, six specific dangers, and three qualities of healthy artistic growth. The anecdote will illustrate several of the dangers at work. The two big ideas will offer a larger framework to help us make sense of what is really dangerous and what is not. The six specific dangers will not be comprehensive, but they will make the point just fine. And I'll end with three qualities of healthy artistic growth because it will be good to envision a positive way forward.

A Personal Anecdote

In the fall of 2002 I wrote and produced a play that we staged at Hope Chapel. It was called "Sarah's Children." Conceived as an Italian family drama set in the time of the Patriarchs, the play was like *The Sopranos* meets *The Ten Commandments*. I wrote the play because as a pastor and an artist I'd had a question I wanted to work out in the context of a Sunday morning: could a forty-five-minute-long work of theater do the work of a sermon? Could the native language of theater affect a transformational encounter with the Word of God? Could it become a parallel to the preaching of a sermon or the administering of the Eucharist?

The previous fall I had produced a play based on Matthew's Gospel. The play had functioned as a conclusion to a teaching series on that same book. People loved it and said,

"Let's do it again!" So we did. Along with a theater friend, Brie Walker, I wrote a piece of historical fiction called "Adam and Eve: In Retrospect." In this work I explored the moment immediately following the fall. What did our two primordial parents talk about? What happened to language? What did it *look like* for their relationship to slowly corrode?

The congregation again received the play enthusiastically and asked if we would do another. So, tipsy with success, I obliged. Hence "Sarah's Children." Six years later my conclusion to the decision to stage this play on Sunday morning is this: I got art wrong and I got church wrong. I foolishly rushed the script, I unwisely chose to perform the first three scenes without any kind of narrative closure, and the play ended abruptly on a dark note of sexual tension between Abraham, Sarah, and Hagar. To top it off, I had to endure a repeat performance in the second service.

The art I had created did not serve the purposes for which the people had gathered. They had gathered to praise God and to be edified by his Word. Instead I had handed them a strange and distracting piece of theater that belonged more properly on a theater stage. The problem was not theater. The problem, indeed the danger, was *this* work in *this* context. The one did not serve the other, so the experiment failed. I sincerely regret my decision. You would be right to pity the leadership of Hope Chapel. I console myself only with the thought that my embarrassing ordeal supplied future generations at Hope with a cautionary tale they won't easily forget.

With this story in mind, let me offer a model that can help us make sense of what actually is a danger and what just seems like a danger.

Two Big Ideas

In the world that God has created there are superordinate Truths and there are subordinate truths. Big T and little t. The superordinate Truths include the essential things we believe about God as Father, Son, and Holy Spirit; our human nature; the church; art. I call them this because they are the truths that fundamentally hold the universe together and make human well being possible. When we get the superordinate Truths wrong, real dangers occur.

What are subordinate truths? The subordinate truths *look* like dangers but in fact are different cultural "skins" in which we live out the big-T truths. They include things like the musical instruments we use in our worship or how we structure our community life or evangelistic efforts. Too often as Christians we confuse the one for the other, the small-t for the big-T truths, and therein derive many of our headaches about art. Let me offer a picture-story.

In the beginning God made twelve tribes of Israel. These twelve tribes had two things in common: they were sons of Abraham and they possessed the Law of Moses. Beyond this they were very different siblings, creatures, cultures—and it seems God liked it that way since he had ordained it.

Now, God made not just human nature to express itself in many ways. He also made physical nature in that manner. He made mountains, plains, tundras, tropics, arctics, savannas, and marine biospheres all of the same stuff of the earth, yet very different in their ecological personalities.

For the sake of our picture-story, let me stick with two "ecological personalities" and let's rename them the Jets and the Sharks. We'll call it the great West Side Story, writ large across the pages of Christendom.

Now the Jets dance in a certain way. They high kick and pirouette on the sidewalk. They twirl with a basketball in hand. They drink sodas and say things like "Let's go daddy-o!" The Sharks, they glide and they strut. Their movements are *suave*. They say things like "Ay caramba!" or "Vamos muchachos!"

The Jets and the Sharks—the white American and the brown Puerto Rican—the desert tribe and jungle tribe—they represent in our picture-story two different church cultures

148

that often do not get each other. The desert tribe, for instance, likes to sing serene hymns. The jungle tribe prefers Palestrina chorales. The shakers and the praise dancers make their moves over against the quiet steps of the Gregorian monks. The Brazilian Pentecostals act out their effusive Easter dramas under the windows of the scholarly German Lutherans. They shout things to each other like:

Jets: "*Your* movie has profanity."
Sharks: "*Your* movie has fake characters."

Jets: "Your physical movements are distracting to the true worship of God!"
Sharks: "Yours deny the incarnation!"

And the shouting rings down through the generations. What is my point? Often it looks like what the other tribe is doing is dangerous. And sometimes it is. Wherever they neglect the superordinate Truths, they will fall into certain danger. But there are times when what they are doing—dancing intensely or sitting deathly—*looks* and *feels* dangerous, yet all that's really happening is that one culture is clashing with another culture while both faithfully enact the gospel.

So my brief pastoral exhortation here is this: Let us be careful in our judgments of each other's artistic experiences. Let us be slow to conclude that they cannot lead to the true knowledge of God. Let us be quick to listen, slow to jump to conclusions, and eager to humbly self-examine our own personalities, our own ethnic and ecclesial cultures, and the ways in which they shape our perception of God and our understanding of what it means to be a disciple of Jesus. We all have plenty to learn about how to be the one body with many, often curious, parts.

Let us now take a brief tour of six real dangers of artistic activity in the church.

149

The Six Dangers

1. Bad art

This is a basic, though not always simple, danger. Bad art, for starters, is cliché, melodramatic, cheap, rushed, plastic, superficialized, elitist, garish, lazy, cold, self-indulgent, and impersonal. Bad art gives you indigestion of the soul, if not also of the body. I have made plenty of my own. And I've witnessed enough to convince me that one of our chief weaknesses as Protestant Christians is that we often do not understand art. Nor are we willing to endure the long years of toil to get it right. We covet the music of George Friedrich Handel. We believe it maximally represents the sounds of heaven. Yet we are often unwilling to make it possible—with money, energy, and time—for one of our own to become a musician of similar ability and influence. So we settle for less.

When I was a child growing up in Guatemala, there was a sweet lady in my church who liked to sing, often, for the whole congregation. When she approached the podium, standing regally before us, she would declaim: "No se leer. No se cantar. No se tocar. Pero para la gloria de Dios!" ("I don't know how to read. I don't know how to sing. I don't know how to play. But for the glory of God!") And that's precisely what we got: a poorly played, poorly sung musical piece that strained our ability to perceive any trace of God's glory. We loved her dearly, and there was no doubt that her heart was in the right place. But her actions betrayed a dismissive view of art that revealed something of her view about God. And, I submit, there is no evidence in Scripture that God pits the sincerity of our hearts over against the excellency of artmaking.

It is one thing, I grant, to make space in your congregation for simple art. Simple art has its good purpose. But it is another thing to call what is bad, good. Often bad art is perpetuated because of ignorance, and sometimes that can turn into pridefulness when we say things like: "We don't *need* to learn what good art is." Now, of course, we want our bridges to be expertly built; we want our doctors to spend years mastering their craft. But art? Well, anybody can make art. And you're right. Anybody can, just like anybody can make LEGO creations or put Band-Aids on a skinned-up knee. But not anybody can make excellent art. That requires just as much skill, experience, and intelligence as industrial engineering or neurology.

My encouragement to us pastors and leaders is to become, slowly but surely, students of good art (to help our congregations mature) and to lovingly steer our artists away from the list of adjectives in the first paragraph (to help them mature).

2. Supersaturation

The world in which most of us live is overstimulating. It looks something like this.

We wake up in the morning to our clock radio. It croons the latest country music tunes, harmonized to updates on weather and traffic. We make it to the bathroom and sit down on our throne. There we flip through the philosophical ruminations of Pottery Barn. Walking into the kitchen, we turn on our morning companion, *Good Morning America*. While we scan the back of cereal boxes for nutritional content, we listen to the latest on Iraq and that wacky, NASA-certified astronaut who drove across the country with a diaper on so she could make like gangbusters on her romantic rival.

We get into our cars and hum down the highway with a cell phone hooked on one ear. We swish by billboards announcing the good news according to the most modern, most *important,* pharmacological research on foot corns. Advertisements dock into our subconscious mind like invisible alien ships.

Throughout the day we indulge in a thousand trivial email exchanges. We knock back a couple of YouTube cocktails. In our regular visits to the grocery store and gas station, we are stalked by an all-pervasive Muzak that makes us feel strangely good about ourselves. We suddenly think, "I'm like a movie star. I too have a soundtrack for my life. I'm *special.*"

151

And when at last we drag our wearied bodies home, we give ourselves just one more glance at the Internet to rummage around for things we think we need, although we're not sure why, when we should be under our covers, eyes closed, mouths shut, prayed up.

As Neil Postman puts it in his book *Amusing Ourselves to Death*, George Orwell feared that what we hate would kill us. But Orwell wasn't right—Huxley was. In his novel *Brave New World*, published in 1932, Aldous Huxley declared that not hate but unremitting pleasure and the "almost infinite appetite for distraction" would destroy us.[2]

If the church perpetuates this state of constant stimulation, whether by means of popular or high art or even of an excess of words, our parishioners will be in danger. As pastors, we will be throwing our lambs to the slaughter. With clogged-up minds and agitated emotions, they will become increasingly vulnerable to the manipulation of media-induced appeals to selfishness. We need to pay careful attention to the ways in which our artistic activity may keep our people in an overstimulated, and therefore morally weakened, state.

3. Estancandose tercamente

Sometimes we get stuck in our ways as churchgoers. Sometimes we get stuck stubbornly. This is what I mean by the Spanish phrase *estancandose tercamente* ("stubbornly stagnating"). Historian Jaroslav Pelikan labeled this the disease of traditionalism, which he described as the dead faith of the living.[3] Consider, for instance, the pipe organ. The organ, some of us believe, is God's instrument of choice (certainly not the electric guitar, which bludgeons the Almighty's ears). But little do we remember that it wasn't until the seventeenth century that the organ was permitted into Reformed church music. In some parts of the fourth-century church, the leadership excommunicated the artist if he insisted that instruments accompany his chanting.

Estancandose tercamente usually sounds like this: "We've always done it this way." Now what's not dangerous is to continue pursuing healthy habits and traditions. These are the gifts our forebears pass on to us for our provision and protection. We've always proclaimed the Nicene Creed. We've always honored the Word of God in our gatherings. These are good things always to be doing. What is dangerous is when we stubbornly close God off from refreshing, redirecting, or even replacing elements in our corporate practice of Christian faith.[4]

4. The utilitarian reduction of art

Some folks deny art any role except as an instrument of service to something perceived to be more important. That service may be to politics (presidential candidate logos) or commerce (Coca-Cola). It can be to the religious activities of the church, such as the children's Sunday school curriculum. In some Christian circles art must have a Bible verse attached to legitimize it. Others say that it is only good art if it is "Christian art," that is, if it is used as a vehicle for evangelism. But if we go down this road far enough, we will begin forcing Bach's *Violin Concerto in A minor* to include vocal annunciations of Jesus's name in order to be God-honoring classical music. If we believe that beautiful things cannot have their own justification for existing, then we might as well say that cherry tomatoes need to be used for evangelism in order to be worth producing.

Cherry tomatoes, of course, *can* be used by Christian organizations like World Vision to provide sustenance to the poor in Christ's name. But before tomatoes are good for Christian purposes they are good for human purposes—in the language of Genesis, "good for food and pleasing to the eye." So, too, before art is good for explicitly Christian service, art is good for human service in general. The danger of limiting art to its utilitarian value is that it belittles the God of all creation. It also robs our artists of a vast terrain of human explora-

153

tion, a terrain with deep sorrows and expansive laughter. The mundane and the mysterious belong to God originally and it is our duty to be good stewards of it all.[5]

To put my point simply: art can wonderfully serve all the functions of the church and we are the richer for it. But when we restrict art to its usefulness to certain church tasks, we make it small. As pastors we will also hurt and lose many of the artists in our communities who feel called to make art for the good of the world at large.

5. Art as a form of distraction

We can use art, like anything else on this planet, to distract ourselves from the hard realities of our lives, or our neighbors' lives. Distraction can become a form of rebellion against God. Let me suggest three ways we might escape through art. First, we can escape into feelings. The feelings we experience during our musical worship, for example, can become a surrogate for the absence of feelings toward God himself. We feel the endorphin rush brought on by the mind-blowing guitar lick. We feel ourselves lifted up. Suddenly we are swelling with intense, throbbing feelings. Is it because of the music or because we've communed with the Spirit of Christ? Often it's just the music. Charismatic churches might especially struggle with this temptation.

Second, we can escape into entertainment, and again our musical worship becomes the setting for this kind of distraction. Coming into a service after a discouraging week, we can feel tempted to want the music to dull our pain. We want to be wowed. We want to be lulled. We want to escape our life, and the music can help us do just that. Seeker-friendly churches might need to be watchful for this temptation.

Finally, we can escape into art itself. We can permit our intensely psychological connection with the artistic work to replace our spiritual connection with God. The choral performance is so "divine," the poetry so sumptuous, that we feel sated with the artistry. We find it easier to stop with the "buzz" than to allow the art to direct our soul to a deeper knowledge of God. Traditional churches of various sorts, whether Presbyterian or Baptist, may find themselves tempted in this way.[6]

Distracting ourselves with art from the concrete reality of a personal God is as dangerous as any other addiction. As leaders we need to keep asking ourselves: Is the art helping people encounter the living God with heart, mind, and body, or is it enabling them to become distracted from him?

6. Good, old-fashioned immaturity

As artists we can become enamored with the margins. We'll drop the f-bomb in order to stick it to The (Religious) Man, as a poet friend once did in my church. We can allow ourselves to be ruled by our emotions. A musician in our community would walk around with a scowl of perpetual indifference, presumably to prove she was a real musician. A lack of self-control can lead us to want to manipulate others. We can hide our sloth or anger under the cape of being an artist. But as hard as it is, we artists need to keep choosing to grow up into the life-giving image of Christ along with the rest of our brothers and sisters.

As leaders we have our own problems. We can be ruled by fear of our congregation, especially of those who have the most money or power. We can refuse to introduce new artistic forms because they will upset the members who want things to stay the same as always. We can do new things simply because they effectively generate numerical growth. Or we can do things that actually cause harm.

I once hosted a discussion of the movie *Magnolia* at Hope Chapel. I firmly believe this film offers one of the most powerful depictions of sin and forgiveness. It is also a disturbing movie, one I do not lightly recommend. I had sent out an email to the whole congregation inviting them to gather on a Monday evening. My goal was to talk about the ideas that filmmaker P. T. Anderson had embedded in his narrative. We would consider their implications for us as Christians. Within a few days of my notice, I received a letter from a man in the congregation. It was eight pages, single-spaced, and livid. In it he told me why what I was doing was wrong. He questioned my character. He said this would be dangerous for the church, especially the young people. His letter made me mad. I had intended something good; here it was backfiring on me. I had never planned to show the movie. I simply wished to discuss it in order to "understand our times."[7]

As it happened, two of our senior pastors called a meeting between myself and this brother. We needed to be reconciled—and we needed help. For over an hour we listened to each other, face-to-face. We explained the reasons for our respective actions. We agreed to disagree on matters where we did not see eye-to-eye. And we gave and received forgiveness. Our senior pastors encouraged us to bless each other. I can't say it was easy. But I learned a valuable lesson. In looking back I realize I was immature. Though my intention was honest, the way I had handled the process lacked sufficient wisdom.

These, then, are six dangers we will encounter as we grow in the amount and intensity of artistic activity in church life. It is important for us to know their names. It is also important to remember what many sixteenth-century Reformers kept clear: *abusus non tolit usum*. The possibility of abuse does not remove the legitimacy of use. Martin Luther put it in earthier terms. People, he said, point out that women and wine are also dangerous things and are being misused. "But what is there that is not being misused?" The question for us, therefore, is not the goodness of art but its specific misuse in the particular contexts of the church, and it is for these misuses that we need to remain alert and discerning.

So with these dangers considered, let us move on to a vision of healthy growth that will help us become wise curators of the arts in our church life.

Three Qualities of Healthy Artistic Growth

To state that the church is constantly growing is to state a truism. The question, as always, is: How do we grow well? Let me suggest three principles that can contribute to healthy growth.

1. Healthy artistic growth is relationally ordered

For the church to experience healthy artistic life, it must choose to order its artistic happenings in a relational manner. As leaders of the church we cannot have good order without relationship. Nor, I believe, can we have good relationship without order. Order without relationship leads to authoritarianism, while relationship without order can become an excuse to be lazy and messy. So we need both: relational order and ordered relationships.

Between whom do we need relational order? First, between pastors and artists. These two need each other far more than they may realize. A pastor, on the one hand, can help the artist to see the big picture of congregational life: the variety of personality types that fills the pews, the importance of patience, the need to honor the context in which the artist seeks to show a work. Artists, on the other hand, can help the pastor comprehend the importance of all our senses—sight, sound, touch, smell, taste—in our communication and reception of the gospel. They can teach us how to understand strange art forms, such as expressionist painting. They can remind us that God is as much a creative Creator as a saving Savior.

We also need good relationship between scholars and practitioners. We need it between the old generation and the new.[8] We need it between our home culture and the cultures far from home. As Lesslie Newbigin rightly insists: "We need the witness of the whole ecumenical family if we are to be authentic witnesses of Christ to our own culture."[9]

None of us on our own, whether pastor or artist, academic or activist, has figured out the whole gospel. God gives us the entire body of Christ, throughout the entire world, to attain fullness of ecclesial life. When pastors and artists defer to each other's strengths and protect each other's weaknesses, the order that results is relationally vibrant.[10] When both pastor and artist humbly seek to know the other as person, not as title or function, the result is God-ordained wisdom. When together they listen on behalf of God's people, it is then that the church has a chance of becoming that holy, fecund body of Christ against which the gates of hell cannot prevail.

2. Healthy artistic growth is contextually relative

Nicholas Wolterstorff offers us a definition for artistic excellence that is helpful to our work of discernment. A work is artistically excellent, he says, if it accomplishes the purpose for which it was created.[11] In our case, the merit of an artistic work in the church is determined by context. Is the context Sunday morning corporate worship? Is it a Wednesday evening informal gathering? Is it an off-campus, sponsored, or unofficial event?

For instance, if you want to discuss at length the redemptive value of horror movies, as I am so inclined, you would probably not use Sunday morning for that purpose. The context does not fit, nor do the people of God expect it. A discussion of believer and filmmaker Scott Derrickson's movie *The Exorcism of Emily Rose* does not accomplish the purpose for which the congregation has gathered: to adore God and to receive the sacraments. A Tuesday night where people come voluntarily is a much more appropriate context. A good question for us pastors and artists to ask is: *Does this particular art best serve the context for which people are gathering?*

A second point is that *excellence* is contextually relative. As an artist I tell my artistic brothers and sisters, "Keep making excellent artwork. The world needs it." As a pastor I might say, however: "Sometimes in the life of the church, aesthetic excellence will not be most important. A different excellency will be needed." For example, I am a fanatic about modern dance. I've little patience for generic, glittery, satiny "praise dancing."

But as much as I value the excellence of professional modern dance, I also realize that sometimes we as a congregation need, for example, to let our children dance before us. They will be anything but nuanced, and some kid will make faces at his mother while another dances to the beat in her own head.

But occasionally we need to remember that the kingdom of God does not belong only to adults. Even as we witness unpolished dancing, *here in our corporate gathering,* we will be reminded that our goal as Christians is not to be polished and impressive, but to be true. The children dancing before the God who in Jesus of Nazareth pulls the little ones into the middle of his preaching reminds us that we are all clumsy, unhinged humans. We too step on others' toes. We too need grace. So the kids' dance becomes not an interruption to the "serious" work of the pastor, but rather an occasion for the gospel to penetrate our hearts with truth.

This doesn't mean we turn our corporate worship into a free-for-all. My point is that, while we seek to offer our best to God and to one another, we must remain intentionally open to the upside-down kingdom in which our notions of excellence may need an occasional refocusing. Most of the time, the skilled dancers will best show us the life of God in the language of dance. Now and then, though, the children will teach us the good news of dancing free and unafraid, just as we are.

What is good artistically, then, is relative to the context in which it is done and why it is done.

3. Healthy artistic growth is organically rhythmed

You and I are creatures of the earth made by a God who established rhythms for the preservation of life. Evening and morning. Summer and winter. Cross and resurrection. These are rhythms in nature and in history, rhythms both physical and spiritual, of plenty and of scarcity. In light of these rhythms, I submit that God has created us to experience the artistic rhythms of *festal muchness* and *cleansing simplicity.* Like so

159

much in our life, our artistic health is a movement across a spectrum, from the maximal to the minimal, back and forth, each playing an important role in our maturation as disciples.

Consider Scripture's witness to festal muchness. In 1 Kings 8:22–53 Solomon prays a dedicatory prayer for the newly built temple. He then throws a party at which he barbecues "so many sheep and cattle that they could not be counted or recorded!" Could not be *counted*? Surely that adds up to an exercise in bovine extravagance. At the wedding in Cana (John 2:1–11), Jesus makes over six hundred liters of wine, far surpassing any notion of need. In God's creation of the universe there are vast surpluses that we cannot reduce to human utility. The seemingly limitless combinations of tasty flavors is but one example: from the fiercely pungent durian fruit to the Toasted Marshmallow Jelly Belly candy.

The Scriptures also commend the practice of cleansing simplicity. "When you fast . . ." Jesus tells his disciples, reminding them that fasting is not an "if" but a "when" (Matt. 6:16). "Deny yourself and take up your cross," he says in Mark 8:35. "I have learned to be content with little," Paul tells the believers at Philippi, and encourages them to learn likewise (Phil. 4:12). All throughout, the Scriptures commend to us a habit of giving ourselves to intentional acts of self-denial for the sake of reorienting our lives. We regularly need our systems cleaned of clutter: noise, busyness, stuff, media, addictive attachments. The practice of cleansing simplicity, to paraphrase Richard Foster, not only cleans us out but brings to light the things that control us.[12]

What might this dual rhythm look like in the artistic life of our churches?

In one season you might choose to display an abundance of visual art: photography, prints, drawings, paintings, textile arts, banners. This bonanza of images will give witness to the graphic splendor of God's creation. In another season you might decide to exhibit only one work. For instance, you place one excellently crafted sculpture at the center of congregational life—maybe at the entrance to the property or in the sanctuary itself. You allow your people to feast on this lone thing for three months, or even an entire year. You let it be long enough for them to feel both the absence of abundance and the tastiness of that one work of beauty.

Or for one very, very long season you build a cathedral. A cathedral. Yes, like the kinds you find scattered throughout Europe. As outrageous as that may sound to our Protestant ears, it is no more outrageous than God's creation of the teeming oceans. Is it worth the time, energy, and expense? That depends on a lot of factors. But we may also ask, are the flora and fish of the seven seas worth the time, energy, and expense? Is the nard that Mary poured over Jesus, valued at a year's labor, worth the time, energy, and expense? Is it worth the *waste*? Jesus's answer to his disciples overturns their assumed notions of worth. Extravagant beauty, whether in creation or in artistic acts, is not the problem. Selfish excess is. So if it seems good to you and to the Holy Spirit (and to the city council), then build a cathedral and let it give glory to God. While you're building your cathedral, commit to give generously to the poor and needy. Make your cathedral a welcoming place for all your neighbors. Make it a gift of great beauty to the city that God so loves.

A last example of this rhythm can be seen in our musical worship. Many of us use multiple instruments to give sound to our worship of God: stringed and percussion instruments, pipe and B-Hammond organs. At our best we celebrate the praise of God with sonic muchness. But what if twice a year we simplified the experience? What if we chose to sing with only one instrument or, dare we propose, none at all? How might that awaken our hearts afresh to God? How might that rescue us from confusing the heart of worship with the instruments of worship? Might it make us notice more the persons alongside whom we lift our praise heavenward? At the very least, giving ourselves to the practice of cleansing

161

simplicity would go a long way toward countering the negative effects of media supersaturation.

In the end, if we only have either festal muchness or cleansing simplicity, we will tire out with too much or too little. While I recognize a relativity among church cultures, in which some will manifest one to a degree more than the other (the gregarious Brazilians versus the reserved Scandinavians), I believe that entering actively into these God-ordained rhythms will lead to the kind of ecclesial well being God has ordained for his people.

Conclusion

As we and our churches grow in our experiences with art, my prayer is that we will not simply fumble toward maturity. I believe God offers us a better way. It involves listening to the wisdom of the family of Jesus that extends across time and space: Gregory the Great's sixth-century chants, the Celts' ninth-century illuminated manuscripts, the French Abbot Suger's twelfth-century church architecture, the fifteenth-century English morality plays, Martin Luther's sixteenth-century hymnody, the Shakers' eighteenth-century dancing. They have conducted their experiments. They have made their mistakes. We do not have to make the same ones. Their wisdom is ours; let us make the most of it. With the Spirit as guide, I am confident that we will find our best growth within the protective care and enthusiastic encouragement of this large family.

Let us risk boldly. Let us fail humbly. Let the Jets among us come fully alive. Let the Sharks become their truthful, God-ordained selves. And let us jointly make such works of artistic beauty—small and large, simple and complex—that the world around us will pause for one moment and say, "Truly there must be a God, and he must be here."

For Further Reading

Harold Best, *Unceasing Worship: Biblical Perspectives on Worship and the Arts* (Downers Grove, IL: InterVarsity, 2003)

Frank Burch Brown, *Good Taste, Bad Taste, and Christian Taste: Aesthetics in Religious Life* (Oxford: Oxford University Press, 2003)

Bill Dyrness, *Visual Faith: Art, Theology, and Worship in Dialogue* (Grand Rapids: Baker Academic, 2001)

Rory Noland, *The Heart of the Artist* (Grand Rapids: Zondervan, 1999)

Gesa Elsbeth Thiessen, ed., *Theological Aesthetics: A Reader* (Grand Rapids: Eerdmans, 2004)

I am including here twelve novels to inspire the imagination of pastors. It is my hope that they will help pastors understand the creative personality of artists a little bit better.

C. S. Lewis, *Perelandra* (New York: Scribner, 1944)

Graham Greene, *The Power and the Glory* (New York: Penguin, 1940)

Shusaku Endo, *Silence*, trans. Monumenta Nipponica (Marlboro, NJ: Taplinger, 1969)

Ron Hansen, *Mariette in Ecstasy* (New York: Harper, 1991)

John Irving, *A Prayer for Owen Meany* (New York: Ballantine, 1990)

Francois Mauriac, *Viper's Tangle*, trans. Gerard Hopkins (Chicago: Loyola Press, 1951)

David Maine, *Fallen* (New York: St. Martin's Press, 2005)

Dorothy Sayers, *Man Born to be King* (Grand Rapids: Eerdmans, 1943)

Marilynne Robinson, *Gilead* (New York: Farrar, Straus, and Giroux, 2004)

Stephen Lawhead, *Byzantium* (New York: HarperCollins, 1996)

Ray Bradbury, *Farenheit 451* (New York: Ballantine, 1953)

Aldous Huxley, *Brave New World* (New York: HarperCollins, 1932)

Phaedra Taylor, "Sam Cherished Cheerfully Golden Moments Calculated." Linocut.

The Future

Looking to the Future: A Hopeful Subversion

JEREMY BEGBIE

Futurology is a foolhardy undertaking, not least when it comes to the arts and Christian faith. I have been asked to look to the future and outline a vision for the church and the arts for the next fifty years. But even if we think only of Europe and North America, the scene is diverse and complex; few would dare to claim they had anything like a comprehensive overview. Moreover, dreams for the future are often wildly unrealistic, needing constant overhauls in the wake of the fumbling failures of fallen human beings.

But there is a danger at a much deeper level, and this is where I want to begin. The commonest way we build a vision for the future is to think *from* the present *to* the future. Our minds move from what *is* to what *will be* or *could be*. This is how futurology generally operates. At any airport bookstall we find titles like *Reading the Times* or *Global Movements That Will Change Your Life*. We are told about the present trends, the vectors of change in our society, the currents that seem to be surging toward the future. There may be a backward glance to a decade or so earlier, but not much further. The main concern is to immerse us in the present in order to envisage what will be or what could be.

The culture-conscious Christian will, of course, be keen to catch these currents, to surf the waves that roll into post-postmodernity. If the church is going to be taken seriously, it cannot afford to imagine the world other than it is. The "emerging church" of the future must resonate with the emerging church today; any other church is doomed to crumble with irrelevance.

But important as "reading the times" may be, if this is the only way we think about the future, we will easily be led down one of two paths. On the one side is *resignation*. We think: "Contemporary culture is going this way, it's in the hands of forces far more powerful than the church, and there's little we can do about it. The best we can do is 'go with the flow' and do our best not to compromise. Or we can simply withdraw from cultural engagement and hang on for heaven." The other path is *triumphalism*. "Contemporary culture is going this way, but we have the power to change it. If only we would believe in ourselves, we could create the future, usher in the kingdom. The future is in our hands, now."

Both paths assume our present determines our future. What *could* be is controlled by what now *is*. I want to suggest that the New Testament writers show a very different mindset. When they present us with a vision for the future, they refuse to move from the present to the future. *They move from the future to the present.* They are captivated above all by a conviction about what God will finally do—the panorama unveiled in Revelation

21 and 22—a future when God will dwell with his people in the new Jerusalem, a future promised by and guaranteed in the raising of Jesus from the dead. And in light of this ultimate hope, they dare to claim that this future can start *now*. They tell us that their lives are being breathed into by the breath of God, being reenergized by God's Spirit, that they are already enjoying the life of the future. The Spirit, they tell us, is the "first fruits" of the final harvest (Rom. 8:23), the "down payment" of what is to come (2 Cor. 1:22; 5:5; Eph. 1:14), the "seal" of the future (1 Cor. 1:21–22; Eph. 1:13; 4:30).

The Spirit is therefore subversive. The Spirit does not simply conform to our present. God's ways are not locked into the present status quo. Things can be different. Resignation is not an option. At the same time, the Spirit does not come to tell us everything is up to us from now on. The Spirit arrives with a vision of a future already assured, and invites us to share in his work of re-creating the present in the light of that future. When the Spirit comes there is subversion, certainly, but a *hopeful subversion*.

If we want a vision for the arts and the church for the next fifty years, this, I suggest, is where we should begin. Not with our present, but with God's future—a future interrupting, erupting into, the present through God's Spirit; a future we do not have to generate out of our own resources, but a future promised by God and available now.

In the light of this future, then, what might the next fifty years look like? What happens when the Spirit comes from the future, and what could this mean for the arts and our churches over the next half century?

We can take all of our cues from the book of Revelation.

The Spirit Unites the Unlike

First, when the Spirit comes from the future, the Spirit *unites the unlike*.

In Revelation 21 we are dazzled by a portrayal of the new Jerusalem, that unnumbered throng of the new heaven and earth. "[God] will dwell with them . . . they will be his peoples" (v. 3). The word "peoples" or "nations" (*laoi*) is indeed plural. John is picking up on the ancient promises of the prophets: that as Israel was to be a light to the nations, so in the end, many nations will stream to worship God.[1] The multiethnic picture is filled out in Acts 2 in the story of the giving of the Spirit on the day of Pentecost. When the Spirit of the "last days" was given, the crowds did not find they spoke the same language; rather, foreigners could understand the disciples in their own languages (Acts 2:6, 8, 11). Ethnic distinctiveness was not overrun; indeed, it seems it was needed. A community of the unlike is born—such is the outcome of the Spirit's work.

Why do I begin here? Because so much contemporary Christianity, especially in the Protestant churches, shows a hankering after *homogeneity*. With such a massive stress on the importance of the undetermined decision of the individual, fortified by a consumer-centered economy, there emerges the strange notion that the Christian church is something I choose in the way I might choose a doctor or dentist—one that meets my needs and causes the minimum of pain. Not surprisingly, the result is church growth by replication; not a community of the unlike, but a community of the like, the community *I like*.

The arts can be quickly drawn into this replicative drive. We find "artistic types" forming their own churches. Or we find churches revolving around music (often simply one brand of it); churches that cater to dance or (more likely) churches that do not; churches that specialize in video art and churches that specialize in hideous art! (A friend of mine describes evangelicals as "the only Christians who can do bad taste with style.") The church dissipates into homogenous zones of cultural or psychological preference, effectively mirroring the late-modern, urban consumerism that surrounds us.

And how might the Holy Spirit subvert this push toward sameness? Supremely, it would seem from the New Testament, by throwing me alongside the stranger (the one I would never have chosen) and taking us both to the foot of the cross. It is on the foundation of the cross that God's countercultural community, the community of strangers, is built. For here, and only here, can the sin that separates us from each other be decisively healed. Only in this way will diversity be saved from divisiveness, difference from confusion. Only in this way will the variety God longs for flourish.

What might this mean for the arts in the church? The symposium out of which the essays of this book have come was a wonderful gathering of the unlike. At its heart was a vision of the meeting of artists and pastors. Quite properly, during our three days together in Austin, we heard much about what artists and pastors have in common. But at the same time, profound differences emerged—not only disagreements (though there were some) but divergent ways of approaching the same realities.

At the risk of gross generalization, artists and pastors tend to feel at home with different media of thought and communication. Pastors spend much of their time crafting spoken and written words, and they will often feel most at ease with the language of declarative statement—what Nicholas Wolterstorff calls "assertoric prose."[2] For example: "Jesus is God and Man," "God is one and three." In grammatical terms, they inhabit the world of indicatives. The chances are that our pastor was trained in the world of indicatives more than any other, so that when he or she talks "theology" with us, this is the kind of language that will be most readily used. And they will often (though not always) tend to be wary of media where such language is absent, or which cannot readily be assimilated to assertoric prose. ("If you can't tell me clearly what that picture means, how can I be sure it means anything at all?")

Artists, on the other hand, naturally gravitate toward different media. In spoken and written language, that will typically mean metaphor, suggestion, allusion, rhyme, and symbol. In nonverbal media, it will mean gesture, color, light and shade, harmony, and so on. Bring artists and pastors together and the result can frequently be mutual incomprehension—and sometimes, sadly, hostility. This is where we need to recall the miracle wrought by the Spirit in Acts 2: the strangers heard each other speak in their own tongues. Substitute "media" for "tongues," and the point will be clear. The British sculptor Henry Moore was once asked by a vicar if he would consider sculpting a piece for a church. Would he *believe* in the subject? Moore replied "Yes, I would. Though whether or not I should agree with your theology, I just do not know. I think it is through art that we artists can come to understand your theology."[3]

Pastors may need to be reminded that artists tend to access, process, and articulate the gospel most readily through the grain of marble and wood, through cadence and meter, and that they may well display a stubborn awkwardness with the prosaic, the definitive, the measured proposition. Artists, for their part, will have to recognize that the kind of language most familiar to the church's theology has proved necessary to the health of the church, and that pastors will often require this kind of language to understand more deeply what the business of art is all about.

At stake here is the health of the body of Christ. In its worship and mission, the church will require different media at different times for different purposes, and these need to be honored for their particular powers. During our Texan gathering, the Spirit was busy subverting our love of homogeneity, refusing to allow artists to talk only to artists or pastors only to pastors, and translating our media so that we could begin to hear each other in our singularities. The Spirit united the unlike for the good of the whole and the good of the future—a hopeful subversion indeed.

But, we should add, the *arts themselves* often have built-in powers which by their very nature can serve to subvert homogeneity. As I have argued elsewhere, most of the arts in one way or another combine or juxtapose the unlike.[4] The key process here is metaphor, and it takes place in multiple ways on multiple levels. In music, for instance, we can find the phenomenon of "polyrhythm"—the simultaneous combination of different rhythms, something which releases an extraordinary energy, far greater than the sum of the parts. Another example is the superimposition of different styles (something made possible by our ability to hear sounds together, "through" each other).[5]

Both of these techniques can be heard in a remarkable CD launched in 1999 called *Simunye*. Two singing groups met in South Africa, the one a vocal ensemble from the University of Oxford, "I Fagiolini," the other a church group, the Sdasa Chorale from Soweto. They engaged in an intensive exchange in order to compare, contrast, and combine their respective musical worlds. They recorded tracks from live worship in churches, studios, and the open air. Here we find music such as Gibbons's "O Clap Your Hands" and medieval motets combined with South African melodies and harmonies. In "Douce Dame Jolie," African cross-rhythms meet the cross-rhythms of 1960s minimalist music to create a remarkable polyrhythmic extravaganza. But perhaps the most striking track is a chant for peace, written during the apartheid era, over which the Oxford singers weave a Gregorian chant setting of the Agnus Dei, the last line being "O Lamb of God who takes away the sins of the world, grant us *peace*." In this way, a political chant for peace is given fresh gospel depth through the liturgical words, and vice versa. Two musical traditions converse without any loss of integrity. And two groups from quite different ethnic backgrounds engage each other. Music's particular powers are being harnessed by the Spirit, generating an unforgettable and infectious energy.

My vision for the arts and the church in the next fifty years? Artists and pastors together discovering the Spirit's unity of the unlike.

The Spirit Generates Excess

Second, when the Spirit comes from the future, the Spirit generates *excess*.

I often find myself gazing at a remarkable painting by Balinese artist Nyoman Darsane, portraying the fertile countryside of his own beloved island. The colors are vastly exaggerated, the lines overelaborated. He is evoking Revelation 22, creation's ultimate future: a perpetual stream, "the river of the water of life" flowing from God's throne, nourishing the trees of life (here, mango trees) on its bank. It is a visualization of excess, the rich, overflowing life of the multidimensional new creation.

What needs subverting here is our common desire for "closed equilibrium." Too often we picture the final future as God simply restoring order, returning things to Eden's happy state. At root we are being trapped by a metaphor (much beloved of the English): that of *balance*. It is as if God were in the business of merely restoring balance to the world, matching x amount of evil with x amount of good, x amount of wrongdoing with x amount of punishment. Behind this, needless to say, lurks an image of God as supremely balanced, flawlessly well adjusted.

But such notions sit uneasily alongside the witness of the New Testament. Here we read of a future that vastly surpasses the Garden of Eden, where evil has not been "balanced out" but defeated by an exceedingly greater love, a future not of lifeless equilibrium but of an infinitely vigorous and uncontainable praise. And this is because the God animating it all is not a God of closed structure but one whose outgoing, inner trinitarian love spills over into the world in boundless grace: a God who provides 180 gallons of wine at Cana, when all they needed was a couple of extra bottles; a God who feeds thousands with bread and fish, but with a surplus of twelve baskets; a God who refuses merely to resuscitate Jesus, restoring him to life only to die again, but gives him

172

a new, uncontainable life that death can never touch.[6] And, moreover, it is this God who now pours out his Spirit so that we can enjoy here and now a foretaste of the abundant future already previewed in Jesus.

Artists should resonate with this very quickly, for in at least two important senses the arts themselves are excessive. First, even though the evidence suggests that the arts have played an important part in human evolution (against those who dismiss them as insignificant froth in evolutionary history), it is hard to argue that the complexities of one of Wagner's music-dramas or the nuances of a Rembrandt self-portrait are biologically necessary, essential to the processes of natural selection.[7] This does not prove that such "excess" issues from a Creator, but it may serve to bear witness, at least, to the God of superabundance made known in Jesus Christ.

The arts tell of excess in another, closely related way: they always "suggest" more than they could ever "tell." The most enriching art is multiply evocative and allusive. This is the difference between a two-dimensional picture on the side of a shoebox and van Gogh's famous painting of worn-down shoes. The latter evokes multiple responses—the earth, trudging, a hard day's toil, and so forth. But no one could ever articulate it all.[8] This is not to say that a piece of art can "mean anything," only that its range of resonances can never be exhaustively specified. As such, art can point to what is true of all our engagement with the world—the world always exceeds our grasp of it. There is a "generative excess" in reality that calls forth and provokes all human inquiry. The arts serve to remind us of this excess, that a purely functional approach to the world (the idea that once one has found a function to something one has fully accounted for it) is narrowly inadequate. The arts remind us of a dimension of "depth in the observable world beyond what is at any moment observable," beyond what is immediately "useful."[9] Again, this does not amount to a knock-down proof of a Creator, but it is highly consonant with belief in a God who himself is generative excess, who lives as generous, excessive love, and who both creates and envelops his creation with this same love. The poet Les Murray speaks of God as "being in the world as poetry / is in the poem, a law against its closure."[10]

But the point can apply to the content or subject matter of the arts. Think, for example, of the way we portray justice. It is not hard today to find Christian artists protesting injustice. And rightly so. But it is much harder to find those who evoke a New Testament vision of justice, where justice is not essentially about balance, calculating crimes on the one hand and meting out an equivalent penalty on the other (though there is of course a place for punishment). New Testament justice goes far beyond retribution and, indeed, far beyond reestablishing a status quo; gospel-shaped justice is aimed at bestowing offenders with an excess of love they could never earn or deserve. Where is this being evoked in contemporary Christian art?

Another example of artistic excess: the radiance of icons. In Revelation 21 and 22, we are told twice that, in the end, there will be no need for the sun or moon, for the Lord God will be the light of all (21:23; 22:5). Eastern Orthodox spirituality celebrates God's "uncreated light," the divine radiance that cannot be contained in the dimensions of space and time, nor ever adequately represented. It is nonetheless evoked in icons, most notably in icons of the transfiguration of Jesus, where God's light interrupts the disciples' world with a glimpse of the future transformation of all things: a hopeful subversion.

My vision for the arts and the church in the next fifty years? Artists and pastors together rediscovering the Spirit's excess.

The Spirit Inverts

Third, when the Spirit comes from the future, the Spirit *inverts*. In the new heaven and new earth, who rules from the throne above but a Lamb?

Not so long ago, I came across Roald Dahl's story "The Upsidedown Mice." An old man lives a simple life in an old house. When mice in the house start breeding, he wants to get rid of them. So he gets some mousetraps and baits them with cheese. Then he puts glue on the underneath of the traps, and sticks them to the ceiling.

That night when the mice came out of their holes and saw the mousetraps on the ceiling, they thought it a tremendous joke. They walked around on the floor, nudging each other and pointing up with their front paws and roaring with laughter. After all it was pretty silly, mousetraps on the ceiling.

The next morning the old man sees the empty traps, smiles, then takes a chair and puts glue on the bottom of its legs and sticks it upside down on the ceiling. He does the same with the TV, the lamp—in fact, everything in the room. We're told he even put a little carpet up there. That night when the mice come out and look up, they are completely baffled.

"Good gracious me!" cried one. "Look up there! There's the floor!"
"Heavens above!" shouted another. "We must be standing on the ceiling."

One by one they begin to feel very dizzy, and panic starts to set in. A very senior mouse with long whiskers takes charge and tells them his plan: "We'll all stand on our heads, then anyway we'll be the right way up." And that's what they do. One by one they all stand on their heads . . . and one by one they pass out from a rush of blood to the brain. When the old man comes down the next morning, the floor is littered with unconscious mice. "Quickly he gathered them up," the story ends, "and popped them all in a basket."[11] The first night, it seemed like a joke. But after the second night, the mice did not assume the room was upside down—they began to wonder whether they were.

What does the Spirit bring from the future? A dizzying, inverted world: the comic world Jesus brought to mind and lived out, where the rich become poor and the poor rich, where the humble are exalted, the exalted humbled. Inversion is also the strategy of much of the book of Revelation, where those who are tempted to see themselves as irrevocably crushed and oppressed by the might of the Roman empire are invited to catch a vision of a wounded Lamb, the one through whom the Creator has defeated the powers of darkness, the one who now shares the Creator's throne and authority. This, not the imperial force of Rome, is the power that belongs to eternity. Just as the mice began to wonder whether the "real" room was the one upside-down, so these tiny churches were made to wonder whether the world opened up by John was the real world. If so, a vast vista of hope was being unveiled.

The Russian philosopher Mikhail Bakhtin has famously written of the phenomenon of "carnival," when medieval towns acted out reversals of social power structures: the village idiot becomes the king, notorious criminals dress up as priests and preach sermons.[12] It may be that some churches will want to consider mounting a "carnival of inversion" today, where the arts can convey a hopeful social subversion. In any case, in contexts of radical injustice, part of the calling of artists will be, like John the Divine, to evoke an overturned world that previews the world to come. It is what the craftsmen of King's College Chapel, Cambridge, offer by placing their stained-glass image of Christ crucified directly above their image of Pontius Pilate. It is what the poet Wilfred Owen poignantly offers in his poem "At a Calvary Near the Ancre," where the dying Christ is portrayed as identifying with the First World War soldiers but far from the religious professionals, the priests and chaplains who were forbidden even to visit the front line. In Owen's mind, a gulf separates those who are "flesh marked by the Beast" (an allusion to Revelation) who "brawl allegiance to the state," and those who quietly "love the greater love" by surrendering their lives.[13] The inversion of worldly importance is subtly reflected in Benjamin Britten's setting of this poem—in the "Agnus Dei" of his *War Requiem*—where, for the first time in the entire work, the liturgical words and Owen's poetry are in complete accord: the liturgy's witness to the "Lamb of God" is allowed to resonate unforgettably with the fate of the hapless and battle-scarred combatants.

My vision for the arts and the church in the next fifty years? Artists and pastors together being stood on their heads by the Holy Sprit, and in *that* way turning the world upside down.

The Spirit Exposes the Depths

Fourth, when the Spirit comes from the future, the Spirit *exposes the depths*.

At the center of John's vision stands the victorious Lamb (Rev. 21:22; 22:3). But earlier he has told us that this Lamb bears the marks of slaughter (5:6). This should stand as a subversive warning against all *sentimentality*: when we misrepresent reality by evading or trivializing evil, usually for the sake of indulging pleasing emotions.[14] Our refusal to face evil for what it is takes many forms, but is perhaps most pointed in Western society's common denial of death. We grab at the things of this world because we cannot bear the thought that they will dissolve into dust like everything else. We dupe ourselves into thinking there will always be enough to meet our wants—enough fuel, enough energy, enough land—because we cannot imagine an end to all our acquiring, the possibility that there are limits, that things and people are not everlasting. Provocatively, theologian Stanley Hauerwas contends, "There's a connection between the amount of money [we] spend on medicine and our reaction to 9/11. Both are attempts to deny that we're not going to get out of life alive."[15]

177

Many believe we have reached an "aesthetic moment" in our culture, when artistic media are quickly assuming massive importance in shaping the Western imagination. If there is truth in this, it is vital that Christian artists do not succumb to the sentimentality that so often accompanies surges of aesthetic enthusiasm. William James once wrote about a visit to a Christian resort in New York State. He tells us of "the atrocious harmlessness of all things" and how he longed for the outside world, with its "heights and depths, the precipices and steep ideals, the gleams of the awful and the infinite."[16] It is probably in our worship that this sentimental "flattening out" is most evident. We see it in our tendency to avoid any art in worship that will not instantly push the "feel-good" button, lest we lose members or repel newcomers. We see it when we insist God should grant everything in an instant, matched by music where every tension is immediately resolved, no dissonance "lived through." We see it when we crave for direct, unmediated access to God, forgetting that God is always to some extent mediated through the finite materials of the created world. We see it in what Rowan Williams calls the "sentimental solipsism" of some recent songwriting, where the erotic metaphors of medieval and Counter-Reformation piety reappear but without the theological checks and balances of those older traditions. As a result, "Jesus as object of loving devotion can slip into Jesus as fantasy partner in a dream of emotional fulfillment."[17]

Of course, great swathes of art, especially of the twentieth century, have waged war against sentimentality—from the Expressionists to Francis Bacon. But we should be wary of presuming too quickly that this will provide the exposure of evil to which the gospel is then presumed to provide the "answer." For in our own power, we can never uncover our true condition. This is the Spirit's work, and he does so above all by returning us repeatedly to Golgotha. Here, climactically and paradigmatically, the Spirit "sounds the depths," and the depths are deeper than any of us could have imagined. Here all pretense is stripped away; here we are all unmasked as enemies of God, murderers of his own only Son. Out of the depths, out of the fathomless abyss to which we have sent him, Christ howls, "My God, my God."

Of course, there is a double exposure here. For the exposure of our true condition is at the same time the exposure of the extent and extremity of God's own love, the sheer strength of divine passion, which precedes and outruns all human sin. For the one who cries from the pit is none other than God himself in solidarity with the lowest of the low; the eternal Son of God dredging the nadir of his creation with patient love; the faithful Son reaching into the pit of darkness we have made for ourselves in order to open it up to his Father's eternal embrace. Here indeed we witness "the gleams of the awful and the infinite": the awfulness of our plight and the ardor of a far greater, infinite love.[18]

Fortunately, many contemporary Christian artists in recent years have found themselves tugging against the strong currents of sentimentality evident in our society: songwriters such as Matt Redman in England;[19] John Bell of the Iona Community;[20] visual artists such as Bruce Herman,[21] Tim High,[22] and Anneke Kaai;[23] the Hungarian playwright Andras Visky.[24] Perhaps rather more "on the edge" are characters such as Sinead O'Connor,[25] the Grammy Award–winning Irish singer and songwriter, whose latest album (entitled "Theology") is dedicated to a professor in thanks for his classes on Jeremiah. Especially prominent in Great Britain is the music of the Roman Catholic composer James Mac-Millan,[26] who embodies perhaps more than any other living musician the counter-sentimentality I am attempting to describe here.[27]

My vision for the arts and the church in the next fifty years? Artists and pastors together exploring what it means to allow the Spirit to "expose the depths."

The Spirit Re-creates

Fifth, when the Spirit comes from the future, the Spirit *re-creates*.

Sadly, much Protestant and Catholic piety has envisaged the Christian's ultimate future in completely nonmaterial terms—often in terms of the release of a nonphysical "soul" from this world (a world presumed to be destined for annihilation in any case) to enjoy the eternal bliss of "heaven," which is pictured as a realm completely other than this world. The New Testament points us to something radically different: a "new heaven" and a "new earth" (Revelation 21 and 22). Here, far from being reduced to nothingness, we find this physical world is not annihilated or thrown away like hopeless trash, but re-created, flooded with the presence of the God who made it. Further, it is not returned to its original, prefallen condition, but raised to a new level of existence. We can look ahead to our world not only liberated from the things which threaten to devastate it, but with a thousand dimensions added, bursting with fresh color and cadences in a wild, limitless, expanding dance of energy.

Far from being conjured up out of nothing or wishful thinking, this vision is earthed in our space and time: in the raising of Jesus from the dead. This physical human being was not returned to his previous condition only to die again, but raised to a new level of life. We can see the Gospel writers struggling to describe it. They write of the risen Jesus being undeniably the same—familiar in appearance, speaking to his disciples, eating breakfast—and yet strangely different—not recognizable at first, able to pass through matter, appear and disappear. Are they not witnessing physical matter, the stuff of Jesus's body, being transformed into the stuff of the new creation?[28] If so, this could hardly be more pertinent for a gathering on "transforming culture." Before we talk about our programs to transform culture, or transform physical matter into things of interest and beauty, it is surely in keeping with the thrust of the New Testament to insist that *the great transformation has already taken place*—behind our backs, so to speak, on Easter morning, itself a promise of the ultimate transformation at the end of history. And instead of talking about ourselves as the prime movers, should we not speak of God inviting us to share in this transformation here and now through his Holy Spirit? Whether through paint or sound, metaphor or movement, we are given the inestimable gift of participating in the re-creative work of the Triune God, anticipating that final and unimaginable re-creation of all matter, space, and time, the fulfillment of all things visible and invisible.[29]

Indeed, if artists and pastors want to begin to set an agenda together for the next few years, they could do much worse than take the notion of creativity and rethink it along these Christ-centered and trinitarian lines, offering a refreshing "hopeful subversion" of an overused and rather tired concept. It would mean we would speak a little less about the artist as creator (which so easily plays into images of artists as quasi gods creating out of nothing) and rather more about the artist as *re*-creator; a little less about creativity and more about *re*-creativity; a little less about creating new worlds and more about sharing by the Spirit God's re-creation of the world he has already made.

Here we only have space to point to just one remarkable piece of art from Mozambique that wonderfully encapsulates the re-creative dynamic I have in mind. Called "The Tree of Life," for a while it was installed in the atrium of the British Museum in London. We recall that "the tree of life" stood inaccessible in the Garden of Eden. In Revelation 22 the tree reappears (as we have already mentioned), growing on the banks of "the river of the water of life" that flows out of the new Jerusalem for the healing of the nations (vv. 1–2). The wonder of this African tree is that it is constructed entirely out of decommissioned weapons from the Mozambique civil war. It would be hard to imagine a more fitting symbol of re-creation, the justice that marks the new world that awaits us. Isaiah's vision of peace comes to mind: when people will beat their swords into ploughshares and their spears into pruning hooks (Isa. 2:4)—and, we might well want to add, their weapons into trees of life.

My vision for the arts and the church in the next fifty years? Artists and pastors together learning the power of re-creation.

The Spirit Improvises

Sixth and last, when the Spirit comes from the future, the Spirit *improvises.*

Perhaps the most striking thing of all about the vision of the new heaven and earth at the end of Revelation is that it is indeed *new.* This is worth probing and pondering carefully. It is new in the sense we have already spoken about: the created world is not returned to its beginning but (like the risen body of Christ) elevated to a fresh level. But it is surely "new" in another sense also—it is *ever* new. In the world to come, nothing ever becomes old, and since it is hard to imagine this as a static state of perfection (if time and movement, as part of God's creation, are taken up in the new heaven and earth), we must surely speak of endless and surprising novelty as belonging to the new creation. We dare to envisage the Holy Spirit weaving limitless, unpredictable improvisations out of the "givens" of creation, doubtless to the delight of us all.[30]

What needs subverting here is the common assumption that there are only two possible basic shapes to our lives— order and disorder. Order is considered good and fruitful; disorder evil and damaging. If our house is immaculate, we are complimented; if it looks like bedlam, we apologize. But are order and disorder the only options? What about laughter? It is not order (predictably patterned) but nor is it disorder (destructive). It is an example of what Daniel Hardy and David Ford call "non-order," or the "jazz-factor."[31]

Those who crave regular order often assume that the only alternative is detrimental disorder. (This is probably why dictators tend to be humorless.) Some church pastors are adept at ordering all the non-order out of life, like Harold Crick in *Stranger Than Fiction*. Worship becomes cleansed of anything remotely spontaneous; church meetings are impeccably prepared and entirely devoid of surprise. Project this onto God, and he becomes the embodiment of order *ad infinitum*, lifeless and dull (as many outside the church believe). But the New Testament opens up to us another dimension of goodness, another dimension of living which exploded into the world on the day of Pentecost, the kind of life we will see in the world to come—the life of the Holy Spirit.

If pastors tend to disparage non-order, creative artists tend to live it and breathe it. After all, even if they are not aiming to be particularly original or novel, their craft to some extent involves the making of the new, that which has not existed before. The problem is that non-order can easily become an end in itself, and (ironically) can flip back into some form of inflexible order remarkably quickly (there is nothing quite as predictable as the weekly "spontaneous" service).

I am caricaturing drastically, of course. But if there is any truth here, we can say this much at least: that one of the reasons artists and pastors need each other is to learn and relearn together that the richest fruit comes from *the interplay between order and non-order*, between the given chords and the improvised riff, between the faithful bass of God's grace and the novel whirls of the Spirit.[32] The question for pastors, then, is: Are you prepared to allow artists room to provoke the church to venture into risky arenas of novelty—a fresh "take" on a parable, a hitherto unexplored zone of culture? The question for artists is: Are you prepared to get to know the "bass lines" of artistic tradition, and, more fundamentally, the bass lines that God uses to hold his church in the faith?

As T. S. Eliot so pointedly asked, How can we be original until we've lived inside a great tradition?[33] How can we even begin to improvise in a way that beguiles our culture until we have something profound to improvise *with*—until we have sat patiently with an Emily Dickinson or a John Milton, with Polanski and Tarkovsky, Scarlatti and Stravinsky? And how can we hope to ensure we are improvising "in the Spirit" unless at the deepest level we are fed by the Scriptures—and by Augustine and Basil the Great, Aquinas and Calvin, Barth and Bonhoeffer?

A foolhardy vision, no doubt, but one that nonetheless seeks to take its energy and inspiration from the Spirit's hopeful subversion, God's future made available in our present.

Of course, none of these dry bones can ever take flesh until we start to sense what artists and pastors sensed many times during that memorable cavalcade in Austin: the Spirit at large, opening us out to each other through words and gestures, conversation and song, speech and silence.

> Slowly I relearn a *lingua*,
> shared overlays of rule,
> lattice of memory and meaning,
> our latent images, a tongue
> at large in an endlessness
> of sentences unsaid.[34]

For Further Reading

Richard Bauckham and Trevor Hart, *Hope against Hope: Christian Eschatology at the Turn of the Millennium* (Grand Rapids: Eerdmans, 1999)

Jeremy Begbie, *Resounding Truth: Christian Wisdom in the World of Music* (Grand Rapids: Baker Academic, 2007)

John W. De Gruchy, *Christianity, Art, and Transformation: Theological Aesthetics in the Struggle for Justice* (Cambridge: Cambridge University Press, 2001)

Jürgen Moltmann, *Theology of Hope* (Minneapolis: Augsburg Fortress, 1993)

N. T. Wright, *Surprised by Hope: Rethinking Heaven, the Resurrection, and the Mission of the Church* (New York: Harper One, 2008)

Jeffrey Guy, "Parable #7." Oil on panel.

Afterword

My Hope and Prayer

For the evangelical Christian community to develop a living artistic tradition, a mulching ground that generates deeper-going artistry which in turn will not be defensive but have staying power, will take a long time. It will probably take more than one generation of artists, art critics, art public, art patrons, art theorists, art publicists, working together in a communal perspective, to develop the normal body for supporting the numerous second-rate artists that are needed to get the few first-rate ones. . . . Perhaps some Christian body, with resources and authority, can enlarge its long-term vision to give priority to such a ministry in the arts, giving support to a gifted artistic community with a united direction and a Holy Spirited vision of compassion for those caught in sin and by evil.[1]

Calvin Seerveld

Without a vision, the man of Proverbs tells us, the people perish (Prov. 29:18 KJV), or as one translation colorfully puts it, the people run wild (NLT). With a vision, the people

187

flourish. The people become all that God has created them to be. I am encouraged by the many people, not just in North America but in England, Germany, Brazil, Thailand, South Africa and around the world, who are today laboring to see the kingdom of God made manifest in all its artistic glory. I am grateful to the many people in the recent past who tilled hard, often lonely ground: Dorothy Sayers and C. S. Lewis in the 1940s and '50s; Francis Schaeffer and Hans Rookmaaker in the '50s and '60s; Madeleine L'Engle in the '70s; Calvin Seerveld and Nicholas Wolterstorff in the '80s and '90s. These and others—Buechner, Shaw, Begbie, Dyrness, Brown, Webber, all Protestant kin—have made it possible for me to come along and find easier labor.[2] I know that plenty of hard work awaits us. Yet I feel very hopeful about our future.

A Hope

What is my hope for us as Protestants? My hope is that we will see churches thoughtfully develop art programs. There is a great need to help our churches discern how the arts can best serve their context and their specific mission. We cannot expect every church to need the kind of art ministry that takes place at Mosaic in Los Angeles or Willow Creek in Barrington, Illinois. But I do wish to see the arts become a normative part of the life of our churches. It will be a marvelous day when children grow up with the mentality that sees art, in all its splendid variety, as a God-given, "normal" part of our Christian faith.

My hope is that we will see a greater number of young Christians entering art schools to pursue careers in the arts. My hope is that some of these men and women will become instructors of the next generation, whether at the USC film program or the Rhode Island School of Design. My hope is that their parents will trust God to help them release their children to enter these demanding but very important environments.

My hope is that a greater number of seminaries will add art-related courses to their curricula. We need to help our future pastors and leaders become artistically literate, to "read" the times, as the sons of Issachar did long ago. In this way they will be able to prepare the people of God to know how to respond to trends—some good, some bad, some neutral—in the art and entertainment arenas. I hope, additionally, to see an increase of graduate institutions producing top-rate scholars in fields related to the arts. Today we have one theologian of culture here (Bill Dyrness), one scholar of liturgical art there (Robin Jensen). We need another twenty like them, working in both confessional and secular universities.

My hope is that parachurch organizations will proliferate to complement the work of the church. In some cases, like Operation Mobilization's ArtsLink, they will provide invaluable resources to the church's cross-cultural mission. In other cases, such as the International Arts Movement in New York City, they will exercise a beautifully allusive influence on the creative community in their city.

My hope is that there will be an increase of involvement in professional societies by believer artists. Some societies will function in a self-consciously, though not heavy-handed, Christian way. They will provide more explicit ways for artists to integrate their art and faith. Pacific Theater Company in Vancouver, British Columbia, represents such a society, as does Christians in the Visual Arts. In other instances, believer artists will choose to work within existing entities: a ballerina dancing with the American Ballet Theater, an entertainment lawyer operating within the Hollywood studio system, a journalist running a very successful rock music magazine.

What will result when we see an increase of these activities? We will witness the development of a greater pastoral maturity, greater artistic maturity, greater theological maturity, greater cultural maturity, and greater professional maturity. With more churches, more artists, more seminaries, more parachurch ministries, and more professional societies involved, we will observe an increase of resources and infrastructure that will enable more artists to acquire greater intelligence, skill, and experience at younger ages, and so create the possibility for a greater number of outstanding artists to emerge from our diverse communities.

My hope, in this vein, is that we as Protestants will recapture a culture of patronage! As Andy Crouch reminds us in his book *Culture Making*, the only way to substantially change culture is to make new culture. Likewise, the only way to substantially change the artistic culture is to make new artistic culture that we believe, directly or indirectly, reflects the life of God's kingdom. We get the culture for which we pay. If we are not willing to spend money, time, and energy to produce new art, and enough of that new art out of which might result a small amount of great art, then we cannot expect the culture around us to change—whether low or high, whether in Seattle or in Salt Lake City. If we are not willing to patronize our artists with practical supports, then we need to think twice about complaining that the culture is going to rot. My hope, however, is that many of us will become excited about the responsibility and privilege of patronage.

What else do I hope for? I hope for an artful cultural cross-pollination. As Christendom in the global South grows strong, the forces of artistic influence will bend northward: from Nigeria to France, from Bollywood to Hollywood. My hope is that as the church of the global South grows it will offer up all its artistic culture to the global North, and that we will be the richer for it.

I also hope to see a fruitful exchange between Christians of different denominations. Presbyterians today devour the writings of Flannery O'Connor. Baptists are listening to the music of Estonian Arvo Pärt, while kids raised in strict Lutheran or Episcopal churches eagerly seek out charismatic worship opportunities. As we experience the new ideas and ways of other Christian communities, we will find our own ideas and ways challenged and refined. The result of this kind of denominational cross-pollination is not only an increase of resources for artists but also a breadth of perspective that can help us create more nuanced, potent art.[3]

If a culture is created for dance in the church, if congregations cultivate a hunger for theologically minded architecture, if film becomes the servant of the contemplative practices of a worshiping body, if poets and theologians come alongside musicians to craft the songs of God's people, if storytellers collaborate with pastors to envision creative ways to embody the mission of God in their towns and cities—well, then, I can only imagine that will be a day of great gospel energy. A lot will depend on our ability to sustain a robust theology of creation. We will need clear-headed ideas about culture. We will want a solid doctrine of the church and a christology that can hold all things together. Plenty will also depend on our humility before God (and our neighbor, of course). But what an exciting time that will be.

A Prayer

I wish to end here by offering a prayer for my fellow pastors and artists. You are gatekeepers in this work of the church. God has entrusted you with great power. You let things in, you keep things out. You do so, frankly, as wisely as you can. As a gatekeeper you play a unique role in this current revival of interest in the arts. I want to pray that God will encourage you in the work you are already doing. The work of pastoring people and of artmaking is hard work, and much of it goes unnoticed. But it is also deeply good work.[4] Both of you are in the business of caretaking and provocation. Both of you need the encouragement of God's people.

Here are some specific things I pray for you:

- I pray that you, pastors and artists, will be far-seeing, courageous shepherds of the church. May God help you discern how to preserve the good of the old and to welcome the good of the new. May you be a shrewd navigator of the magnificent mess that will likely come from our many experiments with the arts.

- I pray that you will help your people resist the dizzying rush of multimedia for its own sake. I pray that you will help them embrace instead a gospel that is artistically full but not manic. May you help your people live well, not simply add more experiences to already busy lives.

- I pray that you will know how to marshal the patrons in your church to invest in artworks that will nourish the world. We need more works like Michaelangelo's *Pietà* and Bach's symphonies that can powerfully reshape the culture for the common good.

- I pray that you will help your community move beyond feeble cultural imitations to aesthetically rich works of art. I pray that you will embrace the slow, patient work that this will require.

- Pastors, may you freely release your artists into the manifold callings upon their lives, wherever these callings may land them. May you equip your artists to enter the larger society to become the incarnational presence of Christ— a presence quietly hidden or boldly prophetic.

- Artists, may you gladly cooperate with the work your pastors are doing to help you find a spiritual home. May your constant desire be to reflect the life of Jesus, holy and whole, humble and content, courageous and fruitful. May you lavish your neighbors with the glory of our Trinitarian God.

May the Spirit guide us—pastors and artists and all who have been summoned to lead and to participate in this mission. May each of us remain faithful to the calling God has placed upon our life and upon the life of our church. And may it give us great joy.

Notes

Introduction

1. The web home for Hope Chapel's arts ministry is http://www.hopearts.org.

2. To be fair, my mother, a concert pianist with high-church sensibilities, did everything she could to instill a love for the fine arts in her children. She was a "holy irritant" against the largely restrictive aesthetics that surrounded me in the culture of our missionary organization.

3. See http://www.chapel.duke.edu.

4. See http://www.byfor.org/project_vancouver.html.

5. Dorothy Sayers, novelist and friend of Lewis and Tolkien writing in the 1950s, put it sharply to Protestants: "The Church as a body has never made up her mind about the Arts, and it is hardly too much to say that she has never tried." If her judgment verges on exaggeration, her lament is nevertheless shared by many of my contemporaries ("Towards a Christian Aesthetic," in *Christian Letters in a Post-Christian World*, ed. Roderick Jellema [Grand Rapids: Eerdmans, 1969], 69).

6. The website for the event still lives at http://www.transformingculture.org.

7. In *The Beauty of God: Theology and the Arts*, ed. Daniel J. Treier, Mark Husbands, and Roger Lundin (Downers Grove: InterVarsity, 2007), 44.

Chapter Two: The Worship

1. For a summary of the program, visit http://www.calvin.edu/worship/grants.

2. For more on this theme, see Robert Wuthnow, *All in Sync: How Music and Art Are Revitalizing American Religion* (Berkeley: University of California Press, 2006).

3. Here and throughout this essay I will use the term "liturgical" to refer to all acts of public worship assembling, regardless of the style of worship. In this sense, both so-called high church and low church Christians are liturgical.

4. Erik Routley, *Christian Hymns Observed* (Princeton: Prestige Publications, 1982), 1.

5. Many organizations, journals, and initiatives of Christian artists— including Christians in the Visual Arts, Christians in the Theater Arts, *Image*, *ARTS (United Seminary)*, and the conference that gave rise to this book— understandably (and wisely) refuse to limit the scope of their work to worship-related arts. The arts have an important role in Christian witness in every arena of life and culture.

6. This brief essay is a kind of rudimentary orientation to a rich and growing literature on the arts in worship. For other recent and forthcoming contributions, see Frank Burch Brown, *Inclusive, Yet Discerning: Navigating Worship Artfully* (Grand Rapids: Eerdmans, 2009); Debra Rienstra and Ron Rienstra, *Worship Words: Discipling Language for Faithful Ministry* (Grand Rapids: Baker Academic, 2009); Eileen Crowley, *A Moving Word: Media Art in Worship* (Minneapolis: Augsburg Fortress, 2006); and Don E. Saliers, *Worship Come to Its Senses* (Nashville: Abingdon, 1996).

7. See, for example, Tod Bolsinger, *It Takes a Church to Raise a Christian: How the Community of God Transforms Lives* (Grand Rapids: Brazos, 2004).

8. To be sure, accessibility is a criterion that has been used to squelch the creativity of many artists. Professional ballet dancers, actors, painters, and sculptors have frequently lived at the margins of congregational life because they have been told their artform is simply too inaccessible to be used in worship. All of the essays in this volume constitute a powerful argument against this kind of marginalization. Congregations would, in most cases, be significantly helped by learning to appreciate a wider and deeper range of artistic expression.

9. This corporate reception is also achieved when congregations are patiently and lovingly taught how to understand and "worship through" a given art form. The experience of public worship, like the experience of museums or baseball games, is infinitely richer when one is guided by perceptive and instructive docents. The best church musicians and artists I know use every available means—church newsletter articles, discussion groups, educational sessions, and more—to wed Christian artistry with Christian education.

10. Brian Wren, "I Come with Joy to Meet My Lord," 1970. Copyright © 1971, Hope Publishing Co., Carol Stream, IL. All rights reserved. Used by permission.

11. Literature in homiletics has recently focused on the significance of the act of listening and feedback in the art of preaching. In a profound way, preaching is not really the act of a single speaker. It is the act of a community, voiced through a designated representative who is formed by that community and accountable to that community.

12. Nancy Chinn and David Philippart, *Spaces for Spirit: Adorning the Church* (Chicago: Liturgy Training Publications, 1998); Catherine Kapikian and Kathy Black, *Art in Service of the Sacred* (Nashville: Abingdon, 2006).

13. See the description of the Iona community in C. Michael Hawn, *Gather into One: Praying and Singing Globally* (Grand Rapids: Eerdmans, 2003), 204–7.

14. For a more extensive account of a covenantal theology of worship, see, for example, Leanne Van Dyk, ed., *A More Profound Alleluia: Theology and Worship in Harmony* (Grand Rapids: Eerdmans, 2005).

15. Nicholas Wolterstorff, *Art in Action: Toward a Christian Aesthetic* (Grand Rapids: Eerdmans, 1980), 184, 188.

16. See Jeremy S. Begbie, "Beauty, Sentimentality, and the Arts," in Treier, Husbands, and Lundin, *The Beauty of God*, 45–69, esp. 56–57.

17. Generating awareness of the problem of sentimentality is one the greatest hazards of work in this field. The risk of offense is astronomically high. One wise strategy is to practice art criticism with a relatively "safe" topic. I have found Frank Burch Brown's illuminating deconstruction of the height (or depth) of sentimentality in the Precious Moments Chapel to serve as one pedagogically useful example in some cultural contexts. See Brown, *Good Taste, Bad Taste, and Christian Taste: Aesthetics in Religious Life* (New York: Oxford University Press, 2000), 138–45.

18. John Calvin, *Commentary on the Psalms* (Grand Rapids: Eerdmans, 1949), commentary on Psalm 9:11. Italics added.

19. John Wesley, *Select Hymns*, 1761. This text is reprinted as a preface in many recently published Methodist hymnals.

20. Greg Scheer, "We Are Waiting," http://www.gregscheer.com/praise/we_are_waiting.html.

21. John L. Bell, "Lift Up Your Heads," copyright 1992 WGRG, Iona Community, Glasgow G2 3DH, Scotland.

Chapter Three: The Art Patron

1. "I went out full, and the Lord has brought me back empty." Papercutting is an art form that became especially popular among eastern European Jews in the seventeenth and eighteenth centuries, as artists began to make elaborate cutouts to decorate legal documents such as marriage contracts.

2. See John Calvin, *Institutes* I.xi.

3. Julia Kasdorf, "Bringing Home the Work," in *The Body and the Book: Writing from a Mennonite Life* (Baltimore: The Johns Hopkins University Press, 2001), 39–47.

4. Louis P. Nelson, *The Beauty of Holiness: Anglicanism and Architecture in Colonial South Carolina* (Charlotte: University of North Carolina Press, 2008), 220–29.

5. See David Morgan, *Visual Piety: A History and Theory of Popular Religious Images* (Berkeley: University of California Press, 1998) and *Protestants and Pictures: Religion, Visual Culture, and the Age of American Mass Production* (New York: Oxford University Press, 1999); Sally M. Promey, "Taste Cultures: The Visual Practice of Liberal Protestantism, 1940–1965," in Laurie Maffly-Kipp, Leigh Schmidt, and Mark Valeri, eds., *Practicing Protestants: Histories of Christian Life in America, 1630–1965* (Baltimore: The Johns Hopkins University Press, 2006), 250–93.

Chapter Four: The Pastor

1. A friend suggested this to me: Do you think that the empty tomb of the resurrection is an echo of the empty Mercy Seat of the Ark? That the two angels in "dazzling clothes" who gave witness to the empty tomb as evidence of resurrection might be an allusion to the two cherubim marking the emptiness that is fullness at the ark? I'd never thought of that before. I'm intrigued. I'm still thinking about it.

Chapter Five: The Artist

1. Josef Pieper, *Only the Lover Sings: Art and Contemplation* (San Francisco: Ignatius, 1990), 31.

2. Pope John Paul II, *Letter to Artists* (Chicago: Liturgy Training Publications, 1999).

3. Thomas Aquinas, *Summa Theologiae* I.xxxix.8.

4. Augustine, *Confessions*, trans. Henry Chadwick (Oxford and New York: Oxford University Press, 2009), I.i.1.

5. Pope John Paul II, *Letter to Artists*.

6. Ibid.

7. William Butler Yeats, *The Trembling of the Veil*, in *The Autobiography of William Butler Yeats: Consisting of* Reveries over Childhood and Youth, The Trembling of the Veil *and* Dramatis Personae (New York: Collier, 1965), 200.

8. Daniel Hoffman, *Poe Poe Poe Poe Poe Poe Poe* (Baton Rouge, LA: Louisiana State University Press, 1998), 33, 46.

9. William Butler Yeats, "What Is 'Popular Poetry'?" in *Early Essays*, vol. 1, *The Collected Works of William Butler Yeats* (New York: Scribner, 2007), 6.

10. Pope John Paul II, *Letter to Artists*.

11. Fyodor Dostoevsky, *The Idiot*, trans. Anna Brailovsky (New York: Random House, 2003), 415.

Chapter Six: The Practitioner

1. Wendell Berry, *The Unsettling of America: Culture and Agriculture*, rev. ed. (San Francisco: Sierra Club Books, 1996), 39.

2. David Bayles and Ted Orland, *Art and Fear: Observations on the Perils (and Rewards) of Artmaking* (Eugene, OR: Image Continuum Press, 2001).

3. Carl Bernstein, "The Idiot Culture," *New Republic*, June 8, 1992, 25, 28.

Chapter Seven: The Dangers

1. John Calvin, *Institutes of the Christian Religion*, ed. John T. McNeill, trans. Ford Lewis Battles (Philadelphia: Westminster, 1960), I.xi.12.

2. Neil Postman, *Amusing Ourselves to Death: Public Discourse in the Age of Show Business* (New York: Penguin, 1985), vii–viii.

3. See in particular *The Emergence of the Catholic Tradition (100–600)*, vol. 1, *The Christian Tradition: A History of the Development of Doctrine* (Chicago: University of Chicago Press, 1971), 7–10.

4. It is also dangerous when we become inordinately attached to an art form as if it were the inviolable Eleventh Commandment.

5. Giving force to this particular danger is a lingering doubt among evangelicals about the goodness of the earth and of culture-making acts. It is the age-old heresy of Gnosticism rearing its ugly head. Andy Crouch, in *Culture Making: Recovering Our Creative Calling* (Downers Grove, IL: InterVarsity, 2008), offers a forceful rebuttal to this heretical mentality.

6. Frank Burch Brown, referring to the *New York Times* music reviewer Bernard Holland, says this: "Having grown up in an Episcopal church and used its classic Book of Common Prayer, he confesses he relished the 'magical imagery and liquid liturgical responses' of Thomas Cranmer's prose, all the while letting the words roll off his tongue without any 'thought to God at all'" ("Is Good Art Good for Christians?" paper delivered at the Conference on Christianity and Literature, September 29, 2007).

7. See 1 Chronicles 12:32.

8. Note Psalm 78:2–4: "I will open my mouth in parables, I will utter hidden things, things from of old—what we have heard and known, what our fathers have told us. We will not hide them from their children; we will tell the next generation" (NIV).

9. Lesslie Newbigin, *Foolishness to the Greeks: The Gospel and Western Culture* (Grand Rapids: Eerdmans, 1986), 146.

10. Echoing John Witvliet's comments in chapter 2, it is crucially important for us pastors to offer ongoing education in the arts: from the pulpit, in adult educational classes, in seminars or small groups. Our congregations *can* learn new artistic languages if they are taught well. And when they do so they open up themselves to a vastly rich way of knowing God.

11. Wolterstorff, *Art in Action*, 157.

12. Richard Foster, *Celebration of Discipline: The Path to Spiritual Growth* (San Francisco: HarperSanFrancisco, 1988), 55. Foster also has a great passage in his book *The Freedom of Simplicity* in which he discusses the tensions churches face with respect to artistic and architectural decisions (*The Freedom of Simplicity* [New York: HarperCollins, 1981], 152).

Chapter Eight: The Future

1. Zechariah 2:10–11; Isaiah 19:25, 56:7; Amos 9:12.

2. Nicholas Wolterstorff, "Afterword," in *Sounding the Depths: Theology through the Arts*, ed. Jeremy Begbie (London: SCM, 2002), 227.

3. As quoted in Walter Hussey, *Patron of Art: The Revival of a Great Tradition among Modern Artists* (London: Weidenfeld and Nicolson, 1985), 24.

4. Jeremy Begbie, *Voicing Creation's Praise: Towards a Theology of the Arts* (Edinburgh: T&T Clark, 1991), 233–55.

5. See Jeremy Begbie, *Resounding Truth: Christian Wisdom in the World of Music* (Grand Rapids: Baker Academic, 2007), 286–94.

6. Easter, we can never forget, is vastly surplus to any "requirement": it is nothing less than the remaking of a dead physical body into something of super-

abundant life. Paul's "spiritual body" of 1 Corinthians 15 is not merely physical but hyperphysical; not merely alive but hyperalive, *excessively* alive.

7. Against Steven Pinker's claims for an "art-making gene" that is naturally selected to impress potential mates, Louis Menand comments: "One suspects that enjoying Wagner, singing Wagner, anything to do with Wagner, is in gross excess of the requirements of natural selection. . . . No doubt Wagner wishes to impress potential mates; who does not? It is a long way from there to *Parsifal*" (http://www .newyorker.com/critics/books/?021125crbo_books).

8. Hilary Brand and Adrienne Chaplin, *Art and Soul: Signposts for Christians in the Arts* (Carlisle, UK: Solway, 2001), 123. This, I think, is what Calvin Seerveld is getting at when he speaks of art's distinctiveness in terms of "allusivity": "Peculiar to art is a parable character, a metaphorical intensity, an elusive play in its artifactual presentation of meanings apprehended" (Calvin Seerveld, *Rainbows for the Fallen World: Aesthetic Life and Artistic Task* [Toronto: Tuppence Press, 1980], 27).

9. Rowan Williams, *Grace and Necessity: Reflections on Art and Love* (London: Continuum, 2005), 154.

10. Les A. Murray, "Poetry and Religion," in *Learning Human: New Selected Poems* (Manchester: Carcanet, 2001), 78.

11. Roald Dahl, "The Upsidedown Mice," in *Puffin Annual Number One*, eds. Treld Bicknell, Frank Waters, and Kaye Webb (London: Puffin Books, 1974).

12. Mikhail M. Bakhtin, *Problems of Dostoevsky's Poetics*, ed. and trans. Caryl Emerson (Manchester: Manchester University Press, 1984), 122–32.

13. Wilfred Owen, "At a Calvary Near the Ancre," in *War Poems and Others* (New York: Random House, 1994), 47.

14. For a more detailed treatment of this, see Jeremy S. Begbie, "Beauty, Sentimentality and the Arts," in Treier, Husbands, and Lundin, *The Beauty of God*, 45–69.

15. http://www.homileticsonline.com/subscriber/interviews/hauerwas.asp.

16. As quoted in William Edgar, *Taking Note of Music* (London: SPCK, 1986), 18.

17. Rowan Williams, "A History of Faith in Jesus," in *The Cambridge Companion to Jesus*, ed. Markus Bockmuehl (Cambridge: Cambridge University Press, 2001), 231.

18. There is, of course, more to say about the resurrection than this; in particular, that it is the transformation of created matter into the conditions of the age to come. But if we are to follow the contours of the New Testament texts, we should *start* with the theme of vindication: the resurrection of Jesus vindicates Jesus as God's anointed, the one in whom sin and death have been defeated once and for all.

To the common objection, "This is to marginalize the resurrection," we must surely respond that in the New Testament, Easter does not cancel the crucifixion but vindicates it, confirms it as *the* place where evil has been grasped and defeated, *the* place where sin is taken to the grave, *the* place where we are both exposed and forgiven.

19. http://www.mattredman.com.

20. http://www.iona.org.uk.

21. http://www.bruceherman.com.

22. http://www.finearts.utexas.edu/aah/studio_art/faculty/high.cfm.
23. http://www.annekekaai.nl/index2.htm.
24. http://www.juliet-tour.com/visky.html.
25. http://www.sineadoconnor.com/biography.htm.
26. http://www.intermusica.co.uk/macmillan.
27. See Begbie, *Resounding Truth*, 176–82.
28. See N. T. Wright, *The Resurrection of the Son of God* (London: SPCK, 2003), pt. 4; *Surprised by Hope* (London: SPCK, 2008), 64–87.
29. For an outworking of this, see Begbie, *Voicing Creation's Praise*, pt. 3; Begbie, *Resounding Truth*, chaps. 8–10.
30. For discussions of this, see Eberhard Jüngel, "The Emergence of the New," in *Theological Essays, Vol. II*, ed. John Webster, trans. Arnold Neufeldt-Fast and John Webster (Edinburgh: T&T Clark, 1995), 35–58; Richard Bauckham, "Time and Eternity," in *God Will Be All in All: The Eschatology of Jürgen Moltmann* (Edinburgh: T&T Clark, 1999), 155–226.
31. Daniel W. Hardy and David Ford, *Praising and Knowing God* (Philadelphia: Westminster Press, 1985), 20, 96–99, 152; see also 119–20.
32. I explore this much more fully in Jeremy Begbie, *Theology, Music, and Time* (Cambridge: Cambridge University Press, 2000), pt. 3.
33. T. S. Eliot, "Tradition and the Individual Talent," in *Selected Essays* (London: Faber & Faber, 1932), 13–22.
34. Micheal O'Siadhail, "Freedom," in *Hail! Madam Jazz: New and Selected Poems* (Newcastle: Bloodaxe Books, 1992), 111.

Afterword

1. In *Bearing Fresh Olive Leaves: Alternative Steps in Understanding Art* (Carlisle, UK: Piquant Editions, 2000), 114.
2. I am equally indebted to many Catholic and Eastern Orthodox writers. I only omit them here because my desire is to draw attention to the specifically Protestant believers who have influenced my thought and life.
3. An entire generation of Protestant believers is being exposed to the riches of historic Christianity. The consequence of this is a whetting of the appetite for substantial, soul-satisfying art. Vineyard rock musicians revisit ancient prayers like "Oh Gladsome Light." Young Methodist seminarians study the iconographic practices of fifteenth-century Russian Orthodoxy. I can only hope that the end result of this development will be a deepening of our ecclesial and artistic identity.
4. Against popular perception, the pastoral and artistic callings resemble each other in many ways. Pastors, for example, have to learn the art, not just the facts, of shepherding people. Artists have to learn how to become good shepherds of the imagination. These are ideas Eugene Peterson explores more extensively in his book *Subversive Spirituality* (Grand Rapids: Eerdmans; Vancouver: Regent College Publishing, 1997).

Contributors

Joshua Banner

Joshua Banner is the Minister of Music and Art and a professor in the Studies in Ministry degree at Hope College in Holland, Michigan. He has degrees in literature and philosophy from Wheaton College and will soon complete a Master of Christian Studies in Interdisciplinary Studies from Regent College, Vancouver. In 1999 he and several other artists created the Backroom Arts community at Bridgeway Church in Oklahoma City. Joshua is a songwriter, recording engineer, worship leader, teacher, aspiring essayist, and husband to the poet Susanna Childress.

Jeremy Begbie

Jeremy is Thomas A. Langford Research Professor of Theology at Duke University Divinity School. He is a Senior Member of Wolfson College and an Affiliated Lecturer in the Faculty of Divinity and in the Faculty of Music at the University of Cambridge. A professionally trained musician, he has lectured extensively in "theology through the arts" in the UK, North America, and South Africa through multimedia presentations. He is author of *Music in God's Purposes*, *Voicing Creation's Praise: Towards a Theology of the Arts*, and *Theology, Music, and Time*.

Andy Crouch

Andy is the author of *Culture Making: Recovering Our Creative Calling*, winner of *Christianity Today*'s 2009 Book Award for Christianity and Culture and named one of the best books of 2008 by *Publishers Weekly*, *Relevant*, and *Leadership*. He is a member of the editorial board of *Books & Culture*. For ten years he was a campus minister with InterVarsity Christian Fellowship at Harvard University. A classically trained musician who draws on pop, folk, rock, jazz, and gospel, he has led musical worship for congregations of as few as five people to as many as twenty thousand. He lives with his family in Swarthmore, Pennsylvania.

Barbara Nicolosi

Barbara has an MA in Film from Northwestern University in Evanston, Illinois. She has been a director of development, a panelist for the National Endowment for the Arts, and a consultant on many film and television projects. She wrote *The Work*, a full-length feature set during the Spanish Civil War, for IMMI Pictures of Beverly Hills. She writes a media column for the *National Catholic Register*, and is on the executive committee of the City of the Angels Film Festival and the board of Catholics in Media. She penned the screenplay for the movie *Mary, Mother of the Christ*.

Eugene Peterson

Eugene was for many years James M. Houston Professor of Spiritual Theology at Regent College, Vancouver. He also served as founding pastor of Christ Our King Presbyterian Church in Bel Air, Maryland. He is probably most well known for *The Message*, his translation of the Bible in the language of today. His other works include *The Contemplative Pastor: Returning to the Art of Spiritual Direction* and *Subversive Spirituality*. Now retired from full-time teaching, Eugene and his wife Jan live in the Big Sky country of rural Montana.

David Taylor

Raised in Guatemala City, David studied at the University of Texas, Georgetown University, the University of Wuerzburg, and Regent College, Vancouver, where he received degrees in theology and New Testament. He is currently a doctor of theology candidate at Duke Divinity School. He was the Arts Minister at Hope Chapel in Austin, Texas, for twelve years. His artistic interests include playwriting and modern dance. He has written for *Books & Culture*, *CIVA Seen*, *Christianity Today*, and *The Christian Vision Project*.

Lauren Winner

Lauren is the author of three books: *Girl Meets God*, *Mudhouse Sabbath*, and *Real Sex: The Naked Truth about Chastity*. She has appeared on PBS's *Religion & Ethics Newsweekly* and has written for *The New York Times Book Review*, *The Washington Post Book World*, *Publishers Weekly*, *Books & Culture*, and *Christianity Today*. The former book editor for Beliefnet, Lauren is Assistant Professor of Christian Spirituality at Duke Divinity School. When she's home in Durham,

North Carolina, you can usually find her curled up, on her couch or screen porch, with a good novel.

John Witvliet

John D. Witvliet is director of the Calvin Institute of Christian Worship and associate professor of music and worship at Calvin College and Calvin Theological Seminary, respectively. His areas of interest include the history of Christian worship, biblical and systematic theology of worship, the role of music and the arts in worship, and consulting with churches on worship renewal. He is the author of *Worship Seeking Understanding: Windows into Christian Practice*, *The Biblical Psalms in Christian Worship*, and editor of *A Child Shall Lead: Children in Worship*.